French
GRAMMAR

11 – 14

Rosi McNab

Heinemann Educational, a division of Heinemann Publishers (Oxford) Ltd.
Halley Court, Jordan Hill, Oxford OX2 8EJ

Heinemann is a registered trademark of Reed Educational and Professional Publishing Ltd

OXFORD MELBOURNE AUCKLAND
JOHANNESBURG BLANTYRE GABORONE
IBADAN PORTSMOUTH NH (USA) CHICAGO

First published 1998

02
10 9 8 7 6

ISBN 0 435 37298 X

Design, typesetting and illustrations by Goodfellow and Egan Ltd, Cambridge

Printed and bound in Great Britain by Bath Press

Contents

1 Nouns

Nouns are 'naming' words. They tell you who somebody is, or what something is:

He's a <u>soldier</u>. There's his <u>mother</u>. It's a big <u>table</u>. Give me that <u>chair</u>.

You can recognise a noun because you can say 'the' or 'a' in front of it:

a pencil   the dog   the houses   the postman   a headache

EXERCICE 1 Which of the following French words are nouns? Think about what each of them means and then write down the numbers of the ones which are nouns.

1 deux	**4** table	**7** Je m'appelle	**9** porte
2 crayon	**5** chaise	Alain.	**10** Au revoir.
3 petit	**6** Bonjour.	**8** livre	

1.1 Masculine, feminine, and how to say 'the'

In French, all nouns are either masculine or feminine.

The word for 'the' in front of masculine nouns is *le*:

le garçon *the boy*   le livre *the book*

With feminine nouns the word for 'the' is *la*:

la fille *the girl*   la porte *the door*

EXERCICE 2 Who are these people? You should be able to work out whether they are masculine or feminine. Write the words out and put either *le* or *la* in front of them.

1 mère	**5** monsieur	**9** fils
2 père	**6** dame	**10** tante
3 grand-père	**7** garçon	
4 grand-mère	**8** fille	

It's not always so easy to tell whether a noun is masculine or feminine. It's not a problem with people but how do you know that a book is masculine or a chair feminine, for example?

When you look a noun up in the dictionary, you will see an *m* or *f* after it to tell you the 'gender', i.e. whether it's masculine or feminine.

house maison (*f*)

pencil crayon (*m*)

You should try to learn the gender of a noun when you learn the actual word. There are clues to help you remember, and some are given on page 7.

EXERCICE 3   Put the correct word for 'the', *le* or *la*, in front of these nouns. They are all objects found in the classroom. (If you don't know what some of the words mean, look them up in a dictionary.)

1 crayon (*m*)	**5** livre (*m*)	**9** table (*f*)
2 fenêtre (*f*)	**6** porte (*f*)	**10** trousse (*f*)
3 calculette (*f*)	**7** sac (*m*)	
4 taille-crayon (*m*)	**8** stylo (*m*)	

EXERCICE 4   Now do the same for these places.

1 maison (*f*)	**5** boulevard (*m*)	**9** parc (*m*)
2 jardin (*m*)	**6** mer (*f*)	**10** place (*f*)
3 garage (*m*)	**7** plage (*f*)	
4 rue (*f*)	**8** magasin (*m*)	

> If the word begins with a vowel or silent **h** you use *l'* instead of *le* or *la*. This makes it easier to say.
>
> hôtel (*m*) – l'hôtel
> auberge (*f*) – l'auberge

EXERCICE 5   Here is a list of places in a town. Put the correct word for 'the', *le, la* or *l'* in front of each of these nouns.

1 appartement (*m*) *flat*	**5** église (*f*) *church*	**9** musée (*m*) *museum*
2 château (*m*) *castle*	**6** mairie (*f*) *town hall*	**10** pont (*m*) *bridge*
3 école (*f*) *school*	**7** gare (*f*) *station*	
4 hôpital (*m*) *hospital*	**8** hôtel (*m*) *hotel*	

EXERCICE 6   Do the same for the next list of ten places.

1 auberge (*f*)	**5** magasin (*m*)	**9** place du marché (*f*)
2 collège (*m*)	**6** marché (*m*)	**10** restaurant (*m*)
3 épicerie (*f*)	**7** parc (*m*)	
4 immeuble (*m*)	**8** piscine (*f*)	

EXERCICE 7   Now do the same with these people and things.

1 arbre (*m*)	**5** homme (*m*)	**9** ville (*f*)
2 bébé (*m*)	**6** horloge (*f*)	**10** village (*m*)
3 eau (*f*)	**7** rivière (*f*)	
4 enfant (*m*)	**8** rue (*f*)	

> The word 'the' and all the words for 'the' in French are called 'definite articles'. Other types of article are explained on pages 8 and 13. You use a definite article to refer to a definite thing. For example, 'the book' means the particular one which we are using or buying, not just any book.

Recognising the gender of nouns – some clues

Nouns which are masculine	Nouns which are feminine

Nouns which are masculine

Male relatives and family members:
 le père, le garçon

Job titles used for men
 (and sometimes women):
 le boulanger, le professeur

Days, months, seasons:
 le deux, le mercredi, le printemps

Weights and measures:
 le kilo

Languages:
 le français, le chinois

Some countries:
 le Japon, les Etats-Unis

Vegetables and fruit not ending in -**e**:
 le chou, le citron

Most words which have been adopted
 from English:
 le short, le walkman

Nouns which end in -**c**:
 le lac

Nouns which end in -**é**:
 le passé

Nouns which end in -**eau**:
 le bateau
 (exception: *eau* = feminine)

Nouns which end in -**ou**:
 le trou

Nouns which are feminine

Female relatives and family members:
 la sœur, la cousine

Job titles used for women:
 la boulangère, la prof, la directrice

Countries and regions ending in -**e**:
 la Russie, l'Allemagne, la Normandie

Rivers:
 la Seine, la Tamise
 (exception: *le Rhône*)

Vegetables and fruits ending in -**e**:
 la carotte, la poire
 (exception: *le pamplemousse*)

Shops:
 la boutique, la boulangerie

EXERCICE 8 Use the rules in the boxes to help you put the correct word for 'the', *le* or *la*, in front of these words.

1 dimanche
2 salade
3 Canada
4 Loire
5 gâteau
6 printemps
7 litre

8 football
9 sac
10 tennis
11 boucherie
12 lundi
13 pâtisserie
14 France

15 hockey
16 marché
17 Dordogne
18 sweat-shirt
19 château
20 français

1.2 How to say 'a'

Just as there are different words for 'the' in French, *le*, *la*, *l'*, there are also two different words for 'a':

the word for 'a' for masculine nouns is *un*:   un sac *a bag*

the word for 'a' for feminine nouns is *une*:   une trousse *a pencil case*

EXERCICE 1   *Sylvie a un frère*. Sylvie has a brother.

Say who else is in Sylvie's family by changing that sentence. Use the correct word for 'a', *un* or *une*.

1 frère	**5** oncle	**9** mère
2 sœur	**6** tante	**10** chien
3 grand-père	**7** père	
4 grand-mère	**8** cousine	

The word 'a', and in French *un* and *une*, are called 'indefinite articles'. You use them to refer to any one item and not a specific one: 'Fetch a book' means any book, not a particular one.

EXERCICE 2   Read what Céline has in her pencil case. Decide whether the words are masculine or feminine and write out two lists: masculine (*un*) feminine (*une*)

> Dans ma trousse, j'ai un stylo, un crayon, une gomme, une règle, un bâton de colle, un clé, un ticket de bus, un compas, une calculette et un taille-crayon.

EXERCICE 3 What has Céline got in her bag? Write out the list using *un* or *une*.

Dans mon sac, j'ai …

1 trousse (*f*)
2 serviette (*f*)
3 tablier (*m*)
4 cahier de maths (*m*)
5 dictionnaire (*m*)
6 short (*m*)
7 tee-shirt (*m*)
8 pomme (*f*)
9 porte-monnaie (*m*)
10 photo (*f*) de mon copain

EXERCICE 4 Copy and complete the sentences, adding the French for 'a'. What do they mean?

1 Passe-moi … règle. (*f*)
   Example: Passe-moi une règle.
   Pass me a ruler.
2 As-tu … gomme? (*f*)
3 Avez-vous … livre? (*m*)
4 Qui a … taille-crayon? (*m*)
5 Faites … brouillon. (*m*)
6 Passe-moi … crayon. (*m*)
7 As-tu … bâton de colle? (*m*)
8 Qui a … sac rouge? (*m*)
9 Je veux … stylo bleu. (*m*)
10 Passe-moi … calculette (*f*), s'il te plaît.

EXERCICE 5 What are they wearing? Write these words out with the correct indefinite article, *un* or *une*. Look up any words that you don't know and remember to check whether they're masculine or feminine.

1 manteau
2 pantalon
3 pull
4 jupe
5 robe
6 chapeau
7 veste
8 anorak
9 tee-shirt
10 sweat-shirt

1.3 Plural nouns

If there is only one of something we say it is 'singular'
or 'in the singular':
one dog

but if there is more than one we say it is 'plural'
or 'in the plural':
two dogs

To make the plural in English we usually add an **-s**:
one dog – two dog**s**
one house – two house**s**

In French, most words make their plural
in the same way, by adding **-s**:
un chien – deux chien**s**
une maison – deux maison**s**

In French, the **-s** is not pronounced when saying the word, so the singular and plural sound the same.

How to say 'the' with plural nouns

For plural nouns, both masculine and feminine, the word for 'the' is *les*.

	singular		*plural*	
m	le crayon	*the pencil*	les crayons	*the pencils*
f	la pomme	*the apple*	les pommes	*the apples*
m	l'homme	*the man*	les hommes	*the men*
f	l'amie	*the girlfriend*	les amies	*the girlfriends*

EXERCICE 1   Put the correct word for 'the', *le*, *la*, *l'* or *les*, in front of these words. First decide whether they are singular or plural.

1 appartements (*m*)   5 arbres (*m*)   9 chambre (*f*)

2 bâtiments (*m*)   6 salle (*f*)   10 magasins (*m*)

3 école (*f*)   7 restaurants (*m*)

4 toilettes (*f*)   8 jardins (*m*)

How to say 'some'

In English, the plural of 'a' is 'some' or 'any':
a cat, some cats

In French, the plural of *un* and *une* is *des*:
un chat, des chats

singular		plural	
J'ai un stylo.	*I've got a pen.*	J'ai des stylos.	*I've got some pens.*
Tu as un stylo?	*Have you got a pen?*	Tu as des stylos?	*Have you got any pens?*
J'ai une pomme.	*I've got an apple.*	J'ai des pommes.	*I've got some apples.*
Avez-vous une pomme?	*Have you got an apple?*	Avez-vous des pommes?	*Have you got any apples?*

You always need that little word *des* in French. Where in English you can say 'We've got apples and oranges', the French equivalent would be:
*Nous avons **des** pommes et **des** oranges.*

EXERCICE 2   Ask an adult if they have a … or any … Use *Avez–vous un / une / des…?*
First decide whether each noun is singular or plural.

1 feutres   4 gomme   7 stylos   9 règles

2 livre   5 crayon rouge   8 calculette   10 trousse

3 feuilles   6 crayons bleus

EXERCICE 3   Now ask a friend if he or she has got a … or any … Use *Tu as un / une / des…?*
First decide which ones are plural.

1 chiens   4 frère   7 hamster   9 cheval

2 sœurs   5 poisson rouge   8 crocodiles   10 oiseau

3 chats   6 lapins

Other plural endings

As you've already seen, most French and English words form the plural by adding **-s**.

There are some English words which make their plural in a different way: foot – feet, sheep – sheep, mouse – mice. They don't follow the usual word patterns.

There are irregular plural forms in French too. Here are some of the most common ones.

A   Most words which end in **-al** form their plural in **-aux** (pronounced 'o'):

un journal	*a newspaper*	deux **journaux**	*two newspapers*
un cheval	*a horse*	deux **chevaux**	*two horses*
un animal	*an animal*	trois **animaux**	*three animals*

B   Most words which end in **-au**, **-eau**, **-eu** and **-ou** add **-x**:

un manteau	*a coat*	cinq **manteaux**	*five coats*
un neveu	*a nephew*	trois **neveux**	*three nephews*
un genou	*a knee*	deux **genoux**	*two knees*

C   Words which already end in **-s**, **-x**, **-z** don't change in the plural:

le bras	*the arm*	les **bras**	*the arms*
le prix	*the price*	les **prix**	*the prices*
le nez	*the nose*	les **nez**	*the noses*

D   Two words which are mostly used in the plural are:

| un cheveu | *a (single) hair* | les **cheveux** | *hair* |
| un œil | *an eye* | les **yeux** | *eyes* |

EXERCICE 4   Put these words into the plural. Use boxes A and B to help you.

1 l'animal
   Example: les animaux
2 l'oiseau
3 le genou

4 le cheval
5 le bateau
6 le journal
7 le château

8 le neveu
9 le jeu
10 le cadeau

EXERCICE 5   Write out the plural forms of these words. Use boxes B and C to help you.

1 le fils (*son*)
   Example: les fils
2 le Français
   (*Frenchman*)

3 l'Anglais (*Englishman*)
4 la croix (*cross*)
5 le repas (*meal*)
6 le feu (*fire*)

7 le bijou (*jewel*)
8 le chou (*cabbage*)
9 le bois (*wood*)
10 la souris (*mouse*)

EXERCICE 6 The next ten words are all parts of the body. Give the plural of each one, using all the rules you have learned for regular and irregular plurals.

1 le bras	**5** le dos	**9** le nez
2 l'œil	**6** la main	**10** le pied
3 l'oreille	**7** le genou	
4 la jambe	**8** le cheveu	

1.4 *Du*, *de la* and *de l'*

The 'partitive article' is the grammatical name for the words we use when we want to indicate 'a part of something' instead of the whole thing. In English we use 'some' or 'any', in French it is *du*, *de la* or *de l'*. It refers to an unspecified quantity such as *du sucre* (some sugar, not a specific amount).

Avez-vous du pain? *Have you got any bread?*
Je voudrais du pain. *I'd like some bread.*

In English we sometimes miss it out altogether. We can say 'I take milk in my tea'. But in French you always have to put it in: *Je prends **du** lait dans mon thé*.

In French 'some' is made up of the word *de* followed by *le*, *la* or *l'*.
Notice that when *de* combines with *le* they become *du*.
De l' is used for both masculine and feminine nouns which begin with a vowel (a, e, i, o, u) or a silent **h**.

de l'ananas
de la confiture
de l'eau
du pain

| *masculine* | de | + | le | = | du |
| | de | + | l' | = | de l' |

| *feminine* | de | + | la | = | de la |
| | de | + | l' | = | de l' |

EXERCICE 1 How would you ask for the items on this list? Add *du*, *de la* and *de l'* to make ten questions.
Start with *Avez-vous …?*
Example: 1 Avez-vous du sucre?

liste de courses

1 sucre (m)
2 pizza (f)
3 gâteau (m)
4 pain (m)
5 sel (m)
6 farine (f)
7 lait (m)
8 tarte aux pommes (f)
9 confiture (f)
10 miel (m)

EXERCICE 2 Offer the following drinks and foods to a French friend. Use *Tu veux …?*
Write out ten questions, adding *du, de la* or *de l'*.

1 jus d'orange
Example: Tu veux du
jus d'orange?
2 lait

3 eau
4 chocolat chaud
5 limonade
6 thé au citron

7 café
8 pain
9 beurre
10 confiture de fraises

EXERCICE 3 Now make a list of what you would say to ask for some of each thing in the
picture. Use *Je voudrais du / de la / de l'*…
Example: Je voudrais du jambon. (I'd like some ham.)

l'eau
la salade
le gâteau
le jambon
le saucisson
le yaourt
la tarte aux fraises
le fromage

De in a negative sentence

Note that when you use *de* in a negative sentence, for example, to say you
haven't got any of something, you use *de* on its own and not *du / de la / de l'*.

masculine	feminine	plural
Je veux **du** café.	Je mange **de la** salade.	Il y a **des** pommes.
I want some coffee.	*I eat salad.*	*There are some apples.*
Je ne veux **pas de** café.	Je ne mange **pas de** salade.	Il n'y a **pas de** pommes.
I don't want any coffee.	*I don't eat salad.*	*There aren't any apples.*

EXERCICE 4 An empty cupboard! Write out ten sentences to say what has run out.
Use *Il n'y a pas de* … (There isn't any …).

1 ketchup
Example:
Il n'y a pas de
ketchup.

2 confiture
3 gâteau
4 sucre

5 lait
6 beurre
7 fromage

8 soupe
9 jus d'orange
10 yaourt

EXERCICE 5 A fussy eater! Write out ten statements saying you don't eat these foods.
Write them in French and then translate them.

1 noix *Example:*
Je ne mange pas
de noix. I don't
eat nuts.

2 bonbons
3 viande
4 poisson

5 laitue
6 tomates
7 légumes

8 pain
9 gâteaux
10 riz

2   Pronouns

A pronoun is a word which stands in for a noun. Instead of saying 'Mr Jones' you can say 'he', instead of saying 'the girl' you can say 'she', and instead of 'my friends and I' you can say 'we'. Pronouns are used to save repeating the same name or thing over and over again.

Pronouns divide up into different groups: subject pronouns, object pronouns (direct and indirect), emphatic pronouns and interrogative pronouns. Don't be put off by the titles – they're all explained in the sections below.

2.1   Subject pronouns

The first group are subject pronouns. These replace the person or thing doing an action. In English they are: I, you, he, she, it, we, they. They are usually used with a verb: I am, you live, he eats, she drinks, it shuts, we have, you go, they talk.

In French they are: *je, tu, il, elle, on, nous, vous, ils, elles.*

As in English, they are used with verbs and they are the 'subject' of the verb – the one doing the action: *je suis, tu habites, il mange, elle boit, nous avons, vous allez, ils parlent, elles jouent.*

	singular		plural	
first person	je, j'	*I*	nous	*we*
second person	tu	*you*	vous	*you*
third person	il	*he/it*	ils	*they*
	elle	*she/it*	elles	*they*
	on	*we/you*		

Je   *Je* becomes *j'* before a vowel or silent **h**, for example, *j'ai, j'habite.* This makes it easier to say. The other thing to remember is that *je* only has a capital J at the beginnning of a sentence. (In English, 'I' is always a capital.)

Nous   *Nous* is the equivalent of 'we': a group of people that includes 'I'.

Tu and vous   In English, we say 'you' whether we're talking to a close friend or a complete stranger and whether there is one person or a group of people.

In French, they make a distinction. There are two words for 'you', *tu* and *vous.*

Tu is used to a single person, someone you know well (a friend or relative) or who is younger than you are.

Vous is used to a group of people, whoever they are.

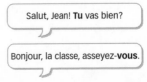

Salut, Jean! **Tu** vas bien?

Bonjour, la classe, asseyez-**vous**.

Vous is often referred to as the 'polite' form as it is also used when talking to someone older than you or a stranger, even if there is only one person (a teacher, your friend's mother or father, etc.).

> Comment allez-**vous**?

If in doubt it is best to use *vous* as *tu* can sound too familiar and it's safest to be polite.

Il and elle

Use these to talk about another person (who is the subject of the verb). Use *il* to say 'he', *elle* to say 'she':

> **Il** s'appelle Gérard. **Elle** a quatorze ans.

Also, remember that all nouns in French are either masculine or feminine. Therefore whenever you want to say 'it' you have to select the correct form, either *il* (masculine) or *elle* (feminine). If the noun you are replacing is feminine (e.g. *une chaise*) then the subject pronoun is *elle*.

> Où est la chaise?

> **Elle** est devant la table.

If the noun you are replacing is masculine (e.g. *un livre*) then the subject pronoun is *il*.

> Tu as mon livre?

> Oui, **il** est dans mon sac.

Ils and elles

Ils and *elles* both mean 'they'. Use *ils* to refer to more than one man or boy, or more than one masculine object.

> Les garçons jouent. **Ils** jouent.

Use *elles* to refer to a group of women or girls or feminine objects.

> Les filles arrivent. **Elles** arrivent.

If you are referring to a group of people or things which are both masculine and feminine you use the masculine form *ils*. You only use *elles* if <u>all</u> the people or things are feminine. So if you have a group of ten girls and one boy, you must still refer to them as *ils*!

Ils sont français.

On

There is one more subject pronoun which you need to be able to recognise: *on*.

On can be used instead of *nous*, especially in informal French:
On va au café? *Shall we go to the café?*

It can be used where in English we would say 'you':
On peut monter à la tour le week-end. *You can go up the tower at weekends.*

It can be used to say 'they' meaning 'people in general':
En France, on conduit à droite. *In France, they drive on the right.*

It always uses the same part of the verb as *il* and *elle*.

EXERCICE 1 Which pronoun do you need to use here?

1 Talking about your friend Martine
  Example: elle
2 Talking about Martine and yourself
3 Asking your teacher a question
4 Talking about a group of boys
5 Talking about your friend Sibylle
6 Talking about your friend Benjamin
7 Talking to your friend Benjamin
8 Talking about your friends

EXERCICE 2 Which pronoun would you use in these sentences? Who or what is the pronoun replacing?

1 Alain habite en France. … habite dans le nord de la France.
2 Paul et Marianne habitent dans le sud. … habitent à Marseille.
3 Moi? … habite à Paris.
4 Où habitez–…, madame?
5 J'habite à Paris avec mes parents. … habitons un grand immeuble.
6 Mélanie et Anne habitent en banlieue. … ont un petit appartement.
7 Ma sœur habite à Lyon. … fait ses études à l'université.
8 Mes grands-parents habitent en Auvergne. … ont une ferme.
9 … habites où, Antoine?
10 Mon frère joue au tennis. … joue très bien.

2.2 Me, you, him, her, it, us, them

Another group of pronouns in English consists of the words me, you, him, her, it, us, them. However, these words can be translated in more than one way in French; in fact there are three groups of pronouns in French that all match up to that group in English. So you need to know which type of pronoun to use when. The three groups are explained below and in section 2.3.

Direct object pronouns

The direct object is the person or thing which has an action done to it. In English you use direct object pronouns all the time without realising. For example, there are two in this sentence: John hit <u>me</u> but the teacher saw <u>him</u>.

EXERCICE 1 Can you spot the direct object pronouns in these sentences?

1 He saw me.
2 I saw him.
3 They saw us yesterday.
4 We see them all the time.
5 I see you.
6 I am looking for her.

In French, the direct object pronouns are: *me, te, le, la, nous, vous, les*.

	singular		plural	
first person	me	*me*	nous	*us*
second person	te	*you*	vous	*you*
third person	le	*him/it*	les	*them*
	la	*her/it*		

When *me*, *te*, *le*, *la* come before a vowel or silent **h**, the **e** or **a** is dropped and they become *m'*, *t'*, *l'*.

In French, you always put the direct object pronoun in front of the verb, so initially it can look quite different from the English version.

Je **la** vois.	*I see **her**.*
Il **nous** voit.	*He sees **us**.*
Ils **te** voient.	*They see **you**.*

EXERCICE 2 Can you put the pronoun into the French translation of each sentence? Use the table above to help you.

1 He sees <u>us</u>. Il … voit.
   Example: Il nous voit.

2 I see <u>him</u>. Je … vois.

3 They see <u>you</u> *(singular)*.
   Ils … voient.

4 We see <u>them</u>. Nous … voyons.

5 I see <u>you</u> *(plural)*. Je … vois.

6 I am looking for <u>her</u>.
   Je … cherche.

7 She is looking for <u>me</u>.
   Elle … cherche.

8 He is looking for <u>me</u>.
   Il … cherche.

9 They find <u>us</u>. Ils … trouvent.

10 We find <u>them</u>. Nous … trouvons.

EXERCICE 3 Spot the direct object pronouns in these English sentences.

1 I like him.

2 Are you listening to me?

3 I like that bag, I'll buy it.

4 John had the ball and he kicked it through the window.

5 We saw him at the station.

6 Can you see her?

7 He's inviting her to his party.

8 My cat catches mice and eats them.

9 I don't like snails, I don't eat them.

10 Look at my new shoes, I wear them all the time.

EXERCICE 4 Now complete the same sentences as in exercise 3 but this time in French, by adding the correct direct object pronoun. Check with the English to see which pronoun to put in. Remember that *me*, *te*, *le*, *la* become *m'*, *t'*, *l'* before a vowel.

1 Je … aime.

2 Tu … écoutes?

3 J'aime bien ce sac, je … achète.

4 John avait le ballon et il … a lancé par la fenêtre.

5 Nous … avons vu à la gare.

6 Vous … voyez?

7 Il … invite à sa boum.

8 Mon chat attrape des souris et … mange.

9 Je n'aime pas les escargots, je ne … mange pas.

10 Regarde mes chaussures neuves, je … porte tout le temps.

Indirect object pronouns

In English, indirect object pronouns are the same as direct object pronouns: me, you, him, her, it, us, them. The only way you can tell the difference in English is if the word 'to' appears or could appear in front of them. When you say 'He gave me the book', you could also say 'He gave the book to me' – 'me' is an indirect object pronoun.

In French, the 'to' is not needed. The pronouns are: *me, te, lui, nous, vous, leur*.

Compare them with the table on page 17. As you can see, they're all the same as the direct object pronouns apart from *lui* and *leur*.

	singular		plural	
first person	me	*to me*	nous	*to us*
second person	te	*to you*	vous	*to you*
third person	lui	*to him/her/it*	leur	*to them*

Me and *te* become *m'* and *t'* before a vowel or silent **h**.

In French, you always put the indirect object pronoun in front of the verb:

Il **me** donne un sandwich. *He gives **me** a sandwich. (He gives a sandwich **to me**.)*
Je **te** donne des frites. *I give **you** some chips. (I give some chips **to you**.)*
Je **lui** donne un livre. *I give **him/her** a book. (I give a book **to him or her**.)*
Nous **leur** donnons les clés. *We give **them** the keys. (We give the keys **to them**.)*
Vous **nous** donnez les lettres. *You give **us** the letters. (You give the letters **to us**.)*

EXERCICE 5 Can you identify the indirect object pronouns in these English sentences?

1 He gives me his pen.
2 I send him a letter.
3 He tells them a story.
4 We buy her a present.
5 You give us the bags.

6 They give him some socks.
7 He gives her some chocolates.
8 You give her your trainers.
9 She lends you her book.
10 I lend them my bicycle.

EXERCICE 6 Then copy out the same sentences in French, filling in the missing pronouns.

1 Il … donne son stylo.
2 Je … envoie une lettre.
3 Il … raconte une histoire.
4 Nous … achetons un cadeau.
5 Vous … donnez les sacs.

6 Ils … donnent des chaussettes.
7 Il … donne des chocolats.
8 Tu … donnes tes tennis.
9 Elle … prête son livre.
10 Je … prête mon vélo.

Direct and indirect object pronouns together

You need to be able to identify the two types of pronoun as they are often used in the same sentence. If you say 'Jane gives it to me', 'it' is a direct object pronoun and 'me' is an indirect object pronoun.

EXERCICE 7 See if you can work out which are the direct and indirect object pronouns in these sentences.

1 I send John the letter. I send it to him.
   Example: direct = it (the letter)
   indirect = him (John)

2 Mark tells the children a story. He tells it to them.

3 Alex and I buy our grandmother a present. We buy it for her.

4 You give us the bags. You give them to us.

5 Alan and Jo give their Dad the socks. They give them to him.

If you want to say this kind of phrase in French you will need to know what order to put the pronouns in.

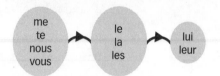

So to say 'I send it to him', as in part 1 of exercise 7, you've got:

| J'envoie | + | la | + | lui |

Check the order of items in the chart above: *la* goes before *lui*, and all pronouns go before the verb, so the correct sequence is:

| Je la lui envoie. |

Study the next three examples and see how they've been worked out.
Il la leur raconte. *He tells it to them.*
Nous le lui achetons. *We buy it for her.*
Elle me l'achète. *She buys it for me.*
(Don't forget that *le* and *la* change to *l'* before a vowel or silent **h**.)

EXERCICE 8 Now have a go at putting the extra pronouns into these sentences in the right order. Then work out what they mean.

1 Marc me donne. (+ la)
   Example: Marc me la donne. Marc gives it to me.

2 Nous la donnons. (+ vous)

3 Hélène et ses parents leur achètent. (+ le)

4 Céline lui achète. (+ les)

5 Kevin et Michel vous donnent. (+ la)

6 Je te prête. (+ les)

7 Mes copains la donnent. (+ me)

8 Le professeur les prête. (+ lui)

9 Vous les achetez. (+ nous)

10 Tu la donnes. + (leur)

2.3 Emphatic pronouns

In phrases like 'He's with me' or 'I did it for him', we use the same set of pronouns again: me, you, him, her, us, you, them. In French, there is a different set of pronouns:

	singular		plural	
first person	moi	*me*	nous	*us*
second person	toi	*you*	vous	*you*
third person	lui	*him*	eux	*them*
	elle	*her*	elles	*them*

These pronouns are only used when talking about people or animals, not objects. Compare this table with the ones on page 17 and page 19. Note that there are different words for masculine and feminine 'them' – *eux* and *elles*.

Use these pronouns for emphasis:
Moi, j'ai 15 ans, et **lui**, il a 14 ans. *I'm 15 and he's 14.*

Use them on their own to answer a question:
Qui a fait ça? **Lui**. *Who did that? Him.*

☞ 6.1 Use them after prepositions (see page 79):
Nous achetons un cadeau pour **eux**. *We're buying a present for them.*

EXERCICE 1 Replace the people who are underlined with the right emphatic pronoun.

1 Jean est allé en ville sans <u>sa sœur</u>.

2 Ma copine est sortie avec <u>ses amies</u>.

3 M. Bertrand a acheté un cadeau pour <u>son oncle</u>.

4 Mon petit ami a mangé avec <u>ma famille et moi</u>.

5 Nous sommes partis sans <u>mes parents</u>.

6 On a acheté des glaces pour <u>toi et tes copains</u>.

If you want to say something belongs to someone, you can use *à* plus an emphatic pronoun:
C'est à moi. *It's mine.*
Ce sac est à toi. *This bag is yours.*

EXERCICE 2 Replace the people who are underlined with an emphatic pronoun.

1 Ce stylo est à <u>Jean-Pierre</u>.

2 Le sac bleu est à Sylvie, et le sac rouge est à <u>Marianne</u>.

3 Ces livres sont à <u>mes parents</u>.

4 La maison est à <u>tes cousins et toi</u>.

5 Le vélo est à <u>mon frère</u>.

6 L'ordinateur est à <u>ma mère</u>.

2.4 Interrogative pronouns

An interrogative pronoun is used to ask the question 'Who?' or 'What?'.

■ To ask about a person, use *qui?* – who?:
Qui dit ça? *Who says that?*
Qui vient à la boum? *Who is coming to the party?*
Qui as-tu invité? *Who have you invited?*

■ To ask about a thing, use the phrase *Qu'est-ce que …?* What (is it that) …?:
Qu'est-ce qu'il dit? *What is he saying?*

■ To use someone's name in a question like that, it's best to give the question with 'he', 'she', etc. and then add the name at the end:
Qu'est-ce qu'**il** dit, **Jean**? *What is Jean saying?*

■ You can also use the short form *que?* (what?) but you need to swap the verb and subject round immediately afterwards:
Que dit Jean? *What is Jean saying?*
Que dit-il? *What is he saying?*

EXERCICE 1 Read each sentence and then ask about the person or thing in brackets. How would you ask the question?

1 (Michel) arrive le premier.
Example: Qui arrive le premier?

2 Jean-Luc porte (un pantalon rouge et un sweat-shirt bleu).
Example: Que porte Jean-Luc?

3 (Thomas) joue au foot.

4 Nathalie dit (la bonne réponse).

5 Jérôme fait (ses devoirs).

6 Nous mangeons (du poisson) ce soir.

7 Vous buvez (de l'eau).

8 (Elvire) va au cinéma.

9 Charlotte lit (une BD).

10 Elle appelle (Thomas) au téléphone.

3 Adjectives

Adjectives are 'describing' words. You use them to say what something is like, they 'describe' a noun.

The water is <u>cold</u>.   or you say: <u>cold</u> water
The children are <u>noisy</u>.   <u>noisy</u> children

 Can you find four adjectives in this speech bubble?

> Thomas est petit. Il est noir et il a les yeux jaunes.
> C'est mon chat préféré.

3.1 Agreement of adjectives: masculine/feminine

☞ 1.1   Remember all nouns in French are either masculine or feminine. (See page 5 to remind yourself how this works.) This is important when using adjectives as the adjective has to 'agree' with the noun it refers to. This means that it may have a different ending when used with a masculine or a feminine noun.

If the noun is masculine, for example, *le garçon*, the adjective used to describe that noun is also masculine, for example, *grand*.

un **grand** garçon *a tall boy*   le garçon est **grand** *the boy is tall*

If the noun is feminine, for example, *la fille*, the adjective used to describe the noun is also feminine.

une **grande** fille *a tall girl*   la fille est **grande** *the girl is tall*

Most adjectives make their feminine form by adding **-e**. Dictionaries often show both forms together, with the **e** in brackets, like this: **bavard(e)**.

masculine	feminine	translation	masculine	feminine	translation
bavard	bavarde	*talkative*	grand	grande	*big/tall*
bruyant	bruyante	*noisy*	intelligent	intelligente	*clever*
chaud	chaude	*hot*	joli	jolie	*pretty*
content	contente	*happy*	lourd	lourde	*heavy*
court	courte	*short*	marrant	marrante	*funny*
étroit	étroite	*narrow*	mauvais	mauvaise	*bad*
fatigué	fatiguée	*tired*	méchant	méchante	*naughty*
fort	forte	*strong*	noir	noire	*black*
froid	froide	*cold*	petit	petite	*small/little*

EXERCICE 1 Copy out these sentences choosing the correct form of the adjectives.

1 Marie est (grand/grande).

2 Sa copine est (intelligent/intelligente).

3 J'habite un (grand/grande) appartement.

4 La rue est (étroit/étroite).

5 La ville est (bruyant/bruyante).

6 L'eau est (froid/froide).

7 Mon copain Sébastien est (bavard/bavarde).

8 Sa sœur est (petit/petite).

9 Mon sac est (lourd/lourde).

10 Le professeur est (fatigué/fatiguée).

Some adjectives already end in **-e**. These do not change for the feminine:
Le garçon est **timide** et la fille est **timide** aussi.

Here are some adjectives which end in **-e** for masculine and feminine:

calme	*calm/quiet*	célèbre	*famous*	difficile	*difficult*
facile	*easy*	faible	*weak*	impossible	*impossible*
jeune	*young*	large	*wide*	malade	*ill*
mince	*thin*	moderne	*modern*	propre	*clean*
sage	*good/sensible*	sale	*dirty*	stupide	*stupid*
timide	*shy*	tranquille	*quiet*	triste	*sad*

EXERCICE 2 Copy out these sentences making the adjectives agree. (Some of the adjectives already end in **-e**!)

1 Cette robe est (sale).

2 Ton frère est (sage).

3 Ta sœur est (bavard).

4 La maison est (grand).

5 La ville est (moderne).

6 Le chanteur est (célèbre).

7 Sa chanson est (triste).

8 Louise n'est pas (content).

9 Son frère est (malade).

10 L'exercice est (facile).

3.2 Agreement of adjectives: plural adjectives

If the noun is in the plural (that is, when there is more than one of something), it usually ends in **-s**, for example, *les garçons*. The adjective describing that noun also has to be plural. For most adjectives, you add an **-s** to the singular form:

	singular	*plural*
masculine	le **petit** garçon	les **petits** garçons
	Le garçon est **petit**.	Les garçons sont **petits**.
feminine	la **petite** fille	les **petites** filles
	La fille est **petite**.	Les filles sont **petites**.

You use the masculine plural form if one of the people or items is masculine, even if all the rest are feminine!

Céline, Delphine et Paul sont **petits**.

EXERCICE 1 Copy out these sentences and make the underlined adjectives plural. Remember some of them are feminine and will need an **-e** as well.

1 Ses frères sont <u>grand</u>.
2 Marianne et Sylvie sont <u>petit</u>.
3 Les enfants ne sont pas <u>content</u>.
4 Les maisons sont <u>moderne</u>.
5 Les pommes frites ne sont pas <u>chaud</u>.

6 Les rues sont <u>étroit</u>.
7 Paul a deux chiens <u>noir</u>.
8 Son copain a des baskets <u>rouge</u>.
9 Les amis de Louise sont <u>jeune</u>.
10 Ses frères et sœurs sont <u>marrant</u>.

EXERCICE 2 Put the correct form of the adjective into each sentence. Find the noun, then decide whether the underlined adjective needs to be masculine or feminine, singular or plural.

1 Isabelle a une <u>petit</u> sœur qui s'appelle Amélie.
2 Elle a deux <u>petit</u> frères qui s'appellent Claude et Maurice.
3 Maurice et Claude sont <u>drôle</u>.
4 Ils ont les cheveux <u>noir</u>.

5 Amélie est très <u>intelligent</u>.
6 Mais elle est souvent <u>méchant</u>.
7 Tous ensemble, Amélie, Claude et Maurice sont <u>bruyant</u>.
8 Isabelle est <u>fatigué</u>. Elle n'est pas <u>content</u>.

3.3 Agreement of adjectives: irregular groups

In French most adjectives make their feminine form by adding **-e** and the plural by adding **-s**. These are called 'regular' adjectives.

However some adjectives do not follow that simple rule. They are called 'irregular' adjectives. They make their feminine and plural forms in different ways, as explained below and on pages 26–28.

-f → -ve

Adjectives which end in **-f** when the noun is masculine change to **-ve** in the feminine. Add an **-s** for the plural.

singular		plural		
masculine	feminine	masculine	feminine	
neuf	neuve	neufs	neuves	*new*
sportif	sportive	sportifs	sportives	*sporty*

Paul est sportif. Sarah est sportive.

-x → -se

Adjectives which end in **-x** when the noun is masculine change to **-se** in the feminine. Note what happens in the plural: the masculine form stays the same while the feminine form adds **-s**.

singular		plural		
masculine	feminine	masculine	feminine	
affreux	affreuse	affreux	affreuses	*awful*
ennuyeux	ennuyeuse	ennuyeux	ennuyeuses	*boring*
heureux	heureuse	heureux	heureuses	*happy*
joyeux	joyeuse	joyeux	joyeuses	*joyful*
paresseux	paresseuse	paresseux	paresseuses	*lazy*
sérieux	sérieuse	sérieux	sérieuses	*serious*

Le garçon est heureux. La fille est heureuse.

But a few adjectives which end in **-x** have their own rules. The best way to cope with this is to learn them straight away.

singular		plural		
masculine	feminine	masculine	feminine	
doux	douce	doux	douces	*soft/sweet*
faux	fausse	faux	fausses	*false/wrong*
vieux*	vieille	vieux	vieilles	*old*

*Before any masculine noun beginning with a vowel (a, e, i, o, u) or silent **h**, *vieux* changes to *vieil*.

un vieil hôtel

Son grand-père est vieux. Sa grand-mère est vieille.

EXERCICE 1 For each sentence, decide on the correct form of the adjective given in brackets.

1 M. Barnard est très (actif).

2 Mme Barnard n'est pas (sportif).

3 Les filles, Marianne et Laure Barnard, sont très (sportif).

4 Les fils, Etienne et Marc, sont (paresseux).

5 Marianne et Laure ne sont pas (heureux).

6 Le film était (ennuyeux).

7 Les chiens sont (heureux).

8 Mon chat est (paresseux).

9 Marilène est (sérieux).

10 Sa peau est (doux).

11 La pollution est (affreux).

12 Ma grand-mère est (vieux).

13 Mes grand-parents sont (vieux).

14 La réponse est (faux).

15 Ces histoires sont (ennuyeux).

16 Mes notes sont (affreux).

-s → -sse
-n → -nne
-l → -lle

For adjectives which end in **-s**, **-n** or **-l**, the feminine form doubles the final letter before adding **-e** or **-es**.

singular		plural		
masculine	*feminine*	*masculine*	*feminine*	
bas	basse	bas	basses	*low*
gros	grosse	gros	grosses	*fat/big*
bon	bonne	bons	bonnes	*good*
ancien	ancienne	anciens	anciennes	*old*
gentil	gentille	gentils	gentilles	*kind/nice*
traditionnel	traditionnelle	traditionnels	traditionnelles	*traditional*

-eau → -elle

A few adjectives end in **-eau**, changing to **-elle** in the feminine. The plural forms add **-x** and **-s** as well.

singular		plural		
masculine	*feminine*	*masculine*	*feminine*	
beau*	belle	beaux	belles	*beautiful*
nouveau*	nouvelle	nouveaux	nouvelles	*new*

Beau and *nouveau* change to *bel* and *nouvel* when they come before a noun beginning with a vowel (a, e, i, o, u) or silent **h**.

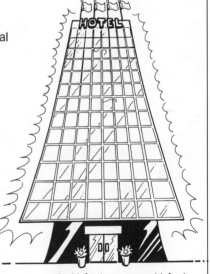

un bel hôtel, un nouvel hôtel

EXERCICE 2 Complete each sentence by filling the gap with the adjective given at the end. Find the noun and put the adjective into the correct form to match it.

1 Mon oncle est … (gros)

2 Ma tante n'est pas … (gros)

3 Ma petite sœur est … (gentil)

4 Mes parents ne sont pas toujours … (gentil)

5 Ma grande sœur est … (beau)

6 Elle a un … chien. (beau)

7 Mes copines sont … (bon)

8 Mes grands-parents sont … (bon)

9 Avignon est une ville … (ancien)

10 Cette chaise est trop … (bas)

11 C'est un livre … (nouveau)

12 Le … hôtel est dans cette rue. (nouveau)

13 Nous avons une … voiture. (nouveau)

14 Mes notes sont … (bon)

15 Quelle … vue! (beau)

-er → -ère

Adjectives which end in **-er** add a *grave* accent in the feminine forms, as well as the extra **-e**.

	singular		plural		
masculine	feminine	masculine	feminine		
cher	chère	chers	chères	*dear/*	
				expensive	
fier	fière	fiers	fières	*proud*	
dernier	dernière	derniers	dernières	*last*	
premier	première	premiers	premières	*first*	

-c → -che/-que

Adjectives which end in **-c** change it in the feminine forms to **-che** or **-que**.

	singular		plural	
masculine	feminine	masculine	feminine	
sec	sèche	secs	sèches	*dry*
franc	franche	francs	franches	*frank*
public	publique	publics	publiques	*public*

EXERCICE 3 Complete these sentences, using the adjective given at the end with its correct ending. Remember to check whether the noun is masculine or feminine, singular or plural.

1 C'est le … jour des vacances. (premier)

2 C'est la … fois que je vais en France. (premier)

3 La semaine … nous avons eu un contrôle. (dernier)

4 As-tu vu le … film de Gérard Depardieu? (dernier)

5 C'est la … tarte aux fraises. (dernier)

6 Mes cheveux sont trop … (sec)

7 J'ai les mains … (sec)

8 Sa chemise est … (blanc)

9 Mes … amis. (cher)

10 Ma … amie. (cher)

11 Mon ami est très … de sa moto. (fier)

12 Ses parents sont très … de lui. (fier)

13 La langue … est parlée en Turquie. (turc)

14 La piscine … n'est pas encore ouverte. (public)

3.4 Adjectives of colour

All colours are adjectives. Most adjectives of colour agree in the same way as other adjectives by adding an **-e** when the adjective is feminine and an **-s** when the adjective is plural.

| singular | | plural | | |
masculine	feminine	masculine	feminine	
noir	noire	noirs	noires	*black*
bleu	bleue	bleus	bleues	*blue*
vert	verte	verts	vertes	*green*

Some adjectives already end in **-e** in the masculine and so do not change in the feminine.

| singular | | plural | | |
masculine	feminine	masculine	feminine	
rouge	rouge	rouges	rouges	*red*
jaune	jaune	jaunes	jaunes	*yellow*
rose	rose	roses	roses	*pink*

Blanc behaves like other adjectives ending in **-c**, changing **-c** to **-che**:

| singular | | plural | | |
masculine	feminine	masculine	feminine	
blanc	blanche	blancs	blanches	*white*

EXERCICE 1 Complete the sentences using the colours given before them. Put the colour into the right form to agree with the noun.

1 (rouge) Sandrine porte une robe …
2 (vert) Ses sandales sont …
3 (gris) Mathieu porte une chemise …
4 (bleu) Sa veste est …
5 (bleu) Kathy porte une jupe …
6 (rouge) Ses chaussures sont …

7 (jaune) Simon porte un tee-shirt …
8 (rouge) Ses baskets sont …
9 (bleu) Jennifer porte un manteau …
10 (jaune) Ses bottes de caoutchouc sont …

EXERCICE 2 Noir(e)(s) ou blanc(he)(s)? Make a list of the clothes in the picture, beginning:
Il y a des chaussettes blanches …

There are some adjectives of colour whose endings never change. The ones you may come across include:

marron	*brown*
chocolat	*chocolate brown*

… and adjectives made up of two words:

bleu marine	*navy blue*
bleu pâle	*pale blue*
bleu clair	*light blue*
bleu foncé	*dark blue*
bleu vert	*blue-green*

EXERCICE 3 Use the right form of the colour adjectives in brackets to complete the sentences.

1 (bleu vert) Séverine a les yeux …

2 (marron) Elle a les cheveux …

3 (bleu marine) Elle porte une jupe …

4 (rose) Elle porte une chemise …

5 (bleu clair) Ses tennis sont …

6 (blanc) Ses chaussettes sont …

3.5 The position of adjectives

When you use an adjective right next to a noun you need to know whether to put it in front of the noun or after it.

Some adjectives come <u>in front of</u> the noun, just as in English:

la **petite** maison *the small house*   le **grand** garçon *the tall boy*

The most common adjectives which come <u>in front of</u> the noun are:

petit *small*   grand *big/tall*   beau *beautiful*   bon *good*   gros *big/fat*
haut *high*   joli *attractive*   long *long*   mauvais *bad*   vieux *old*

However most adjectives come <u>after</u> the noun:

la maison **moderne** *the modern house*   le garçon **marrant** *the amusing boy*

Sometimes you'll see a noun with one adjective before and one after it:

un **petit** livre **intéressant** *an interesting little book*

EXERCICE 1 Before or after the noun? Decide by checking the box above and write them out correctly. Then give the meaning in English.

1 une montagne (haute)
   Example: une haute montagne
   (a high mountain)

2 un enfant (sage)

3 un oiseau (petit)

4 une vue (belle)

5 un garçon (paresseux)

6 un château (vieux)

7 une idée (bonne)

8 une histoire (intéressante)

9 une fille (jolie)

10 un livre (gros)

11 un bâtiment (moderne)

12 un voyage (long)

13 une expérience (mauvaise)

14 une ville (grande)

15 des chaussettes (blanches)

16 un chat (petit/noir)

Some adjectives actually have two meanings depending on their position. They have a completely different meaning if they are used before or after the noun. These adjectives are surprisingly common, so you need to know them.

un **cher** ami *a dear friend*
un pull-over **cher** *an expensive pullover*

un **ancien** élève *a former pupil*
une ville **ancienne** *an old town*

mes **propres** mains *my own hands*
les mains **propres** *clean hands*

ce **pauvre** enfant *that poor child i.e. unhappy*
une famille **pauvre** *a poor family i.e. not rich*

le **seul** homme au monde *the only man in the world*
l'homme **seul** près de la porte *the man alone / on his own by the door*

EXERCICE 2   Before or after the noun? Put the adjective in the right space so that the sentence makes sense. Then say what it means in English.

1 Je l'ai vu de mes … yeux … (propres)

2 Ce soir je vais vous présenter, … auditeurs … , une émission sur la santé. (chers)

3 Il y a un rendez-vous pour les … élèves … (anciens)

4 Je n'ai pas un … jean … à me mettre, ils sont tous sales. (propre)

5 Les … pulls … sont en laine. (chers)

6 Le guide nous montre la/l' … ville … (ancienne)

7 Ces … enfants … qui dorment dans la rue. (pauvres)

8 Les … gens … n'ont pas de voiture. (pauvres)

9 Répétez l'exercice, c'est la … solution … (seule)

10 Il y a beaucoup de … personnes … de nos jours. (seules)

3.6 Possessive adjectives

Possessive adjectives are words which tell you who something belongs to: my coat, his pen, your book, their house, our cat, and so on.

In English, we only have one form for each person: my, your, his, her, our, their. In French, there are different forms for each person and you have to use the right one depending on the noun – masculine, feminine or plural. In other words, the possessive adjective has to agree with the noun it relates to.

This is a complete table of the possessive adjectives. Each line of the table is explained in more detail in the sections below.

masculine	feminine	plural	
mon	ma	mes	my
ton	ta	tes	your (tu)
son	sa	ses	his/her/its
notre	notre	nos	our
votre	votre	vos	your (vous)
leur	leur	leurs	their

My – mon, ma, mes

Let's look at the word for 'my' first. The word for 'my' agrees with the person or thing it is describing. This means that you use the masculine form *mon* with masculine nouns:

Mon frère s'appelle John. *My brother is called John.*

J'ai perdu **mon stylo**. *I've lost my pen.*

... the feminine form *ma* with feminine nouns:

Ma sœur s'appelle Elisabeth. *My sister is called Elisabeth.*

C'est **ma trousse**. *That's my pencil case.*

... and the plural form *mes* with plural nouns:

Mes parents s'appellent Greg and Sue. *My parents are called Greg and Sue.*

Mes tennis sont dans le sac. *My trainers are in the bag.*

EXERCICE 1

Mon, *ma* or *mes*? Copy out the words adding the correct word for 'my' before each one. The gender is given to help you: *m* = masculine, *f* = feminine, *pl* = plural.

1 stylo (*m*)
    Example: mon stylo
2 gomme (*f*)
3 feutres (*mpl*)

4 trousse (*f*)
5 sac (*m*)
6 tennis (*fpl*)
7 serviette (*f*)

8 livres (*mpl*)
9 règle (*f*)
10 crayons (*mpl*)

EXERCICE 2   Imagine this is a picture of your family. A friend asks you who each person is: *Qui est-ce?* Use the words in the box to help you answer the question for the people and pets in the photo. Say: *C'est …* or *Ce sont …*

| père | mère | sœurs | frère | grand-père | cousin | cousine | chat | chiens |

Attention, mes amis!
With feminine nouns that begin with a vowel (a, e, i, o, u), you use the masculine form *mon* rather than *ma*, to make it easier to say. So, for example:
mon amie = *my friend (female)*
mon ami = *my friend (male)*

If there is another word before the noun, such as *petit(e)*, then you use *ma* again:
ma petite amie = *my girlfriend*
mon petit ami = *my boyfriend*

EXERCICE 3   Write out these words with the correct word for 'my' before each one.

1 copain	4 copines	7 amis	9 petit ami
2 copine	5 ami	8 amies	10 petite amie
3 copains	6 amie		

Your – *ton, ta, tes*   The words for 'your' when talking to a friend behave in the same way as *mon*, *ma*, *mes* and even rhyme with them.

You use *ton* with masculine nouns: **ton stylo** *your pen*
… *ta* with feminine nouns: **ta trousse** *your pencil case*
… and *tes* with plural nouns: **tes tennis** *your trainers*
You also use *ton* with a feminine noun beginning with a vowel or silent **h**:
ton amie *your friend (female)*

EXERCICE 4   Imagine that a friend is asking you if you can recognise members of his family. He shows you the photo in exercise 2 and asks: *Qui est-ce?* (Who is it?). You answer using *C'est ton …* or *C'est ta …* or *Ce sont tes …* for the people and pets in the photo.

EXERCICE 5 The next ten questions are addressed to you personally. Copy them out adding *ton*, *ta* or *tes* in the gap. Then answer the questions using *mon*, *ma* and *mes*.

1 Comment s'appelle … ami(e)?
Example: Comment s'appelle ton ami? Mon ami s'appelle John.

2 Comment s'appelle … grand-mère?

3 Comment s'appelle … grand-père?

4 Comment s'appelle … prof de maths? (*m* or *f*)

5 Comment s'appellent … frères et sœurs?

6 Comment s'appelle … chat?

7 Comment s'appelle … chien?

8 Comment s'appelle … prof de français? (*m* or *f*)

9 Comment s'appelle … chanteur ou … chanteuse préféré(e)? (*m* or *f*)

10 Comment s'appelle … groupe préféré? (*m*)

His and her – *son, sa, ses*

If you want to say 'his brother' or 'her brother' you say *son frère*.

If you want to say 'his sister' or 'her sister' you say *sa sœur*.

If you want to say 'his parents' or 'her parents' you say *ses parents*.

son frère

son frère

In French, it doesn't matter whether you're talking about a boy or girl, a man or a woman, the possessive adjective agrees with the noun (thing or person) that belongs to the person you are talking about. Use *son* for a masculine noun, or a feminine noun beginning with a vowel or silent **h**. Use *sa* for a feminine noun. Use *ses* for a plural noun.

EXERCICE 6 Parlez-moi de Thomas. Here are ten facts about Thomas and his family. Complete them by adding *son*, *sa* or *ses* before each noun.

1 … mère est infirmière.

2 … père travaille dans une banque.

3 … sœur travaille aussi à l'hôpital.

4 … frère est grand.

5 … petite sœur est gentille.

6 … cousin s'appelle Auban.

7 … amie s'appelle Juliette.

8 … sport préféré est le tennis.

9 … plat préféré est la pizza.

10 … couleur préférée est le rouge.

EXERCICE 7 Parlez-moi de Charlotte. Now do the same for Charlotte. Remember the words for 'her' are the same as those for 'his' – *son*, *sa*, *ses*. They agree with the noun they go with.

1 … amie s'appelle Jennifer.

2 … petit ami s'appelle Benjamin.

3 … frère s'appelle Nicolas.

4 … sœur s'appelle Isabelle.

5 … parents s'appellent Fred et Margaret.

6 … chien est petit et noir.

7 … chambre est grande.

8 … couleur préférée est le bleu.

9 … plat préféré est le poulet-frites.

10 … boisson préférée est le jus de mangue.

Our – *notre, nos*

The word for 'our' for a single item or person is *notre*. It is the same for both masculine and feminine, but changes to *nos* in the plural.

notre appartement, notre maison, nos enfants

EXERCICE 8

How would you say these are 'our' things? Start with *C'est* or *Ce sont* and then add *notre* or *nos* before the noun.

1 maison (*f*)	3 chambre (*f*)	7 chaises (*fpl*)
Example: C'est notre	4 lits (*mpl*)	8 livres (*mpl*)
maison.	5 armoire (*f*)	9 voiture (*f*)
2 appartement (*m*)	6 commode (*f*)	10 ordinateur (*m*)

Your – *votre, vos*

 2.1

The words for 'your' in the polite or plural form (the *vous* form – see page 15 if you want to check the difference between *vous* and *tu*) are easy to remember because they rhyme with *notre* and *nos* and behave in the same way.

votre appartement, votre maison, vos enfants

EXERCICE 9

Imagine you're speaking to an adult and need to know if these family members and items belong to them. For each one, ask *C'est votre …?* or *Ce sont vos …?*

1 frère	5 chats (*mpl*)	9 maison (*f*)
2 parents	6 immeuble (*m*)	10 affaires (*fpl*)
3 sœur	7 sac (*m*)	
4 copine	8 stylo (*m*)	

Their – *leur, leurs*

If something belongs to two or more people, you use 'their' in English, for example, 'That's their house, across the street'. In French, you use *leur*:

leur maison *their house*   leur fille *their daughter*

You need to add an **–s** if the noun is plural:

leurs enfants *their children*

EXERCICE 10

The items listed below belong to a whole family. Write out a sentence for each one, using *C'est leur …* or *Ce sont leurs …*

1 voiture	2 garage	5 fleurs
Example: C'est leur	3 bicyclettes	6 chien
voiture.	4 jardin	7 cochons d'Inde

EXERCICE 11 Write a caption for each picture. Start with *C'est* or *Ce sont*, then add the correct possessive adjective (using the English as a clue) and finally the word for the noun. *Example: 1 Ce sont ses chiens.*

his	her	their	your

your	our	my	your

3.7 Asking 'which?' – *quel*?

'Which' is called an 'interrogative adjective', because it asks a question (= interrogative) about a noun. For example, 'Which book do you mean?' 'Which person?' 'Which shops?'

The French equivalent is *quel* but the spelling changes to agree with the noun.

	singular		plural	
	masculine	*feminine*	*masculine*	*feminine*
	quel	quelle	quels	quelles

Quel monsieur est le plus grand? *Which man is the tallest?*

Quelle femme habite à Paris? *Which lady lives in Paris?*

Quels enfants jouent dans la rue? *Which children are playing in the street?*

Quelles pommes sont les moins chères? *Which apples are cheapest?*

EXERCICE 1 Quel look préfères-tu? Insert the correct form of *quel* to complete the questions.

1 … pantalon (*m*) préfères-tu?
Example: Quel pantalon préfères-tu?

2 … chemise (*f*) préfères-tu?

3 … chaussures (*fpl*) préfères-tu?

4 … short (*m*) préfères-tu?

5 … sweat-shirt (*m*) préfères-tu?

6 … veste (*f*) préfères-tu?

7 … chaussettes (*fpl*) préfères-tu?

8 … tennis (*fpl*) préfères-tu?

9 … jean (*m*) préfères-tu?

10 … baskets (*fpl*) préfères-tu?

EXERCICE 2 Write down the questions you would ask at school to be sure you're doing the right thing. Give the meaning in English too.

1 salle de classe (*f*)

   Example: C'est quelle salle de classe?

   Which room is it?

2 professeur (*m*)

3 matière (*f*)

4 livre (*m*)

5 page (*f*)

6 exercices (*mpl*)

EXERCICE 3 Add *quel*, *quelle*, *quels* or *quelles* to complete these questions and then say what they mean.

1 … heure est–il?

2 … est la date de ton anniversaire?

3 … temps fait–il?

4 … jour?

5 … ligne de bus?

6 … est ta matière préférée?

7 … est ton plat préféré?

8 … sont tes émissions préférées?

9 … sont tes passe-temps préférés?

10 … couleur préfères-tu, le bleu ou le rouge?

3.8 Demonstrative adjectives

Demonstrative adjectives point out a particular person or thing. In English, we say 'this', 'that', 'these' or 'those': this boy, these boys, that girl, those girls.

In French, you use *ce*, *cet*, *cette*, *ces*, depending on the noun.

* *Cet* is used for masculine words which begin with a vowel (a, e, i, o, u) or silent **h**, to make them easier to say: *cet appartement*, *cet hôpital*.

masculine	**ce** livre	*this/that book*
	cet hôtel*	*this/that hotel*
feminine	**cette** fille	*this/that girl*
plural	**ces** enfants	*these/those children*

EXERCICE 1 Decide whether the noun is masculine, feminine or plural and then add *ce*, *cet*, *cette* or *ces* to each sentence.

1 Je vous recommande … hôtel.

2 Derrière … maison, il y a un grand jardin.

3 Dans … jardin, il y a beaucoup de plantes exotiques.

4 … personnes travaillent dans le jardin.

5 … fleurs sont rares.

6 … arbre est très ancien.

7 … porte est pour les visiteurs.

8 … dépliants sont gratuits.

EXERCICE 2 Do the same again: add *ce*, *cet*, *cette* or *ces* to these sentences.

1 As-tu vu … bébé?

2 … enfant est méchant.

3 … monsieur est grand.

4 … homme est le mari d'Antoinette.

5 Regarde … garçon qui joue au tennis.

6 … filles chantent bien.

7 … ados jouent de la guitare.

8 … messieurs vont au travail.

9 … femme habite près de chez moi.

10 … agent de police a eu un accident.

If you want to distinguish more strongly between 'this girl here' and 'that girl there', you can add *-ci* for 'here' and *-là* for 'there':

cette fille-ci, cette fille-là *this girl (here)*, *that girl (there)*

Ces garçons-ci parlent français et ces garçons-là parlent espagnol.
These boys speak French and those boys speak Spanish.

EXERCICE 3 How would you say the following in French?

1 this girl here   5 these children here   9 that flat there

2 this man here   6 that man there   10 those shops there

3 this dog here   7 that woman there

4 these books here   8 that car there

EXERCICE 4 Fill the gaps with *ce*, *cet*, *cette*, *ces* and *-ci* or *-là*, to distinguish between these people and things. Then translate the sentences into English.

1 … rues … sont étroites, … rues … sont larges.

Example: Ces rues-ci sont étroites, ces rues-là sont larges.

These streets here are narrow, those streets there are wide.

2 … gâteau … est petit, mais … gâteau … est cher.

3 … appartement … est au deuxième étage, … appartement … est au cinquième.

4 … chien … est grand, … chien … est petit.

5 … livre … est plus intéressant, … livre … est moins intéressant.

6 … voitures … coûtent cher, … voitures … coûtent moins.

3.9 Comparisons

In English, you can use 'comparative adjectives' to compare two things – for example, to say that something is 'bigger than' or 'smaller than' something else.

In French, you can do the same thing, adding the word *plus* (more) or *moins* (less) to make the comparison.

Nicolas est grand. Ludovic est **plus grand**. *Nicolas is tall. Ludovic is taller.*
Simon est bavard. Mélanie est **moins bavarde**. *Simon is chatty. Mélanie is less chatty.*

Watch out for agreement of the adjective. The adjective still agrees with the noun it describes. Can you spot the masculine and feminine adjectives in this example?

Le CD est cher, la vidéo est plus chère, et la cassette est moins chère.
The CD is dear, the video is dearer, and the cassette is less expensive.

EXERCICE 1 Complete the following sentences to make comparisons. Remember to add *plus* or *moins* and to repeat the adjective, making sure that it agrees with the noun.

First say that these are all 'more ...':

1 Le petit garçon est timide mais sa sœur est ... *Example: plus timide*

2 Notre maison est grande mais votre maison est ...

3 Gilles est marrant mais sa sœur est ...

4 Cet exercice est difficile mais le prochain exercice est ...

5 L'histoire est intéressante mais la BD est ...

Now say that these are all 'less ...':

6 La Mercedes est chère et la Citroën est ...

7 La jupe bleue est longue et la jupe noire est ...

8 Cette émission est intéressante mais l'autre est ...

9 Le lac 'A' est profond et le lac 'B' est ...

10 Gilles est timide mais sa sœur est ...

To say that something is bigger or smaller <u>than</u> something else you use *que*:

Il est **plus grand que** moi. *He is taller than me.*

Il est **moins grand que** son frère. *He is shorter (less tall) than his brother.*

To say that two things are similar, you use the expression *aussi ... que*, meaning 'as ... as'.

Il est **aussi grand que** son père. *He is as tall as his father.*

Il est **aussi méchant que** son frère. *He is as naughty as his brother.*

EXERCICE 2 Use the adjective *grand* and the word in brackets to make comparisons between the people in each sentence. Remember to make *grand* agree with the noun. Then translate them.

1 Mon frère est ... ... que ma sœur. (moins)
   Example: Mon frère est moins grand que ma sœur. My brother is shorter than my sister.

2 Mon père est ... ... que ma mère. (plus)

3 Lucille est ... ... que son copain. (plus)

4 Benjamin est ... ... que son frère. (aussi)

5 Mes grands-parents sont ... ... que mes parents. (moins)

6 Ellie est ... ... que Noémi. (aussi)

EXERCICE 3 Now make comparisons using the adjectives and symbols in brackets. Remember to make the adjective agree with the noun where necessary.

Key to symbols:

– moins … que

+ plus … que

= aussi … que

1 Mon grand-père est … … … ma grand-mère. (+ vieux)

2 Nicholas est … … … son frère. (= marrant)

3 Paris est … … … Lyon. (+ grand)

4 Le mont Everest est … … … le mont K2. (+ haut)

5 La Seine est … … … la Loire. (– long)

6 Le lac d'Annecy est … … … le lac du Bourget. (– grand)

7 En Provence il fait … … … en Normandie. (+ chaud)

8 L'après-midi il fait … … … la nuit. (– froid)

9 La vue de la montagne est … … … la vue du lac. (= beau)

10 Le footing est … … … le yoga. (+ fatigant)

Using the superlative

This title sounds very grand but in fact it just means saying something is 'the biggest' or 'the smallest', 'the best' or 'the worst', and so on.

In French, you add a word for 'the' before the comparative adjective (see page 38), i.e. you put *le, la, l'* or *les* before *plus/moins …*

Nicolas est **grand**, Ludovic est **plus grand** mais Stéphan est **le plus grand**.

Nicolas is tall, Ludovic is taller but Stéphan is the tallest.

Marianne est **petite**, Sarah est **plus petite** mais Florence est **la plus petite**.

Marianne is small, Sarah is smaller but Florence is the smallest.

La montagne **la plus haute** du monde s'appelle mont Everest.

The highest mountain in the world is called Mount Everest.

EXERCICE 4 Complete this list to say who is the tallest, the smallest, the most chatty, etc., in this class. Remember to make the adjectives agree.

Dans notre classe …

Germaine + grand   Nathalie + bavard   Ishmaïl + marrant

Joseph + intelligent   Edith + petit   Julie + sportif   Boris + paresseux

EXERCICE 5 Now complete these sentences using *le plus …/la plus …* and the adjective given in brackets, making it agree with the noun.

1 La montagne … … … d'Europe est le mont Blanc. (haut)

2 Le fleuve … … … de la France est la Loire. (long)

3 La grotte … … … s'appelle le puits d'Aphanize. (profond)

4 La stalagmite … … … se trouve dans l'Armand. (grand)

5 Le glacier … … … d'Europe s'appelle le glacier d'Argentière. (long)

6 Le lac naturel … … … … de France est le lac du Bourget. (grand)

Good, better, best

The adjective *bon* (good) follows its own rules for comparisons. You don't need the word *plus*. The word *meilleur* replaces *bon* instead. There is a similar change in English: we say 'good – better – best'. In French, it's *bon – meilleur – le meilleur*. There are feminine and plural forms:

	singular		plural		
masculine	feminine	masculine	feminine		
bon	bonne	bons	bonnes	*good*	
meilleur	meilleure	meilleurs	meilleures	*better*	
le meilleur	la meilleure	les meilleurs	les meilleures	*best*	

Simon est **bon** acteur, mais Thomas est **meilleur**.
Simon is a good actor, but Thomas is better.
Boris est le **meilleur** élève de la classe. *Boris is the best pupil in the class.*
Sandrine est la **meilleure** élève de l'année. *Sandrine is the best pupil in the year.*

EXERCICE 6 Add (*le/la/les*) *meilleur/meilleure/meilleurs/meilleures* to complete these sentences. Remember to check whether the noun is masculine or feminine, singular or plural.

First say something is 'better than' something else:

1 Mes notes sont … en français qu'en allemand.

2 Ma montre est … que ta montre et moins chère!

… and now say something is 'the best':

3 La vue d'ici est … … de la région.

4 Ce château est … … exemple d'un château fort en France.

… and now talk about 'my best …':

5 Ma … copine s'appelle Isabelle.

6 Voici mes … photos de nos vacances.

7 C'est mon … stylo. Ne le perdez pas!

8 J'ai invité mes … copains à ma boum.

4 Verbs

Verbs are 'doing' words. They say what you do or are doing, or what someone or something else is doing:

I <u>read</u> a lot. He <u>watches</u> television. My sisters <u>are eating</u>.

When you look a verb up in a dictionary, you will find the infinitive: 'to read', 'to watch', 'to eat'. This is the 'name' of the verb. In English, the infinitive usually starts with 'to'.

lire *verb* to read

EXERCICE 1 Here are some French infinitives. See how many you can match up with the English infinitives. Write them out in pairs. *Example: parler = to speak*

parler
habiter   jouer   regarder
écouter   porter   travailler
manger   laver
aimer

to wash
to listen   to like
to live   to eat   to watch
to speak   to wear   to play
to work

What are the last two letters of each of the French infinitives above? They are important because the last two letters tell you which group the verb belongs to. Those 10 verbs are all in the group of **-er** verbs.

There are three main groups of verbs in French: their infinitives end in **-er**, **-ir** and **-re**. Over 80% of verbs belong to group 1, but you need to know about all three groups.

group 1 -er verbs	group 2 -ir verbs	group 3 -re verbs
for example jouer regarder	for example finir dormir	for example répondre écrire

'Regular' verbs fit into those three groups. 'Irregular' verbs don't – they have their own patterns.

The 'stem' or 'root' of the verb is the part which is left after you take off the last two letters. The stem helps you to form other parts of the verb, so it's important to know how to find it.

EXERCICE 2 What is the stem of each verb in this list?

1 vendre (*to sell*)
   Example: vend-

2 montrer (*to show*)

3 parler (*to speak*)

4 sortir (*to go out*)

5 laver (*to wash*)

6 finir (*to finish*)

7 écouter (*to listen*)

8 dormir (*to sleep*)

4.1 The present tense: -er verbs

We use the present tense to say what you are doing now or what is happening now. In English, we have two kinds of present tense, to say what is happening now and to say what happens usually:

1 I <u>am reading</u>. They <u>are working</u>. It <u>is raining</u>.

2 I <u>read</u> a lot. They <u>work</u> hard. It <u>rains</u> often.

In French, there is one present tense, used to say what is happening now and also what usually happens. *Ils travaillent* could be translated as 'they are working' or 'they work'.

Verbs change according to who or what is doing the action. Look at the box below to see how the verb *parler* (to speak) changes.

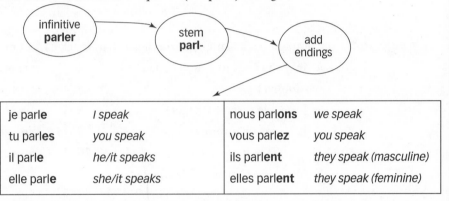

je parl**e**	*I speak*	nous parl**ons**	*we speak*
tu parl**es**	*you speak*	vous parl**ez**	*you speak*
il parl**e**	*he/it speaks*	ils parl**ent**	*they speak (masculine)*
elle parl**e**	*she/it speaks*	elles parl**ent**	*they speak (feminine)*

To make the present tense, start with the <u>infinitive</u>, take off the last two letters to find the <u>stem</u> of the verb, and add the right <u>ending</u> according to who or what you are talking about.

Talking about yourself: I – *je*

If you are talking about yourself in English, you use the 'I' form, or 'first person singular'. In French, this is the 'je' form, and for **-er** verbs you add **-e** to the stem.

infinitive		*first person singular*	
aimer	*to like*	j'aime	*I like*
danser	*to dance*	je danse	*I dance*
écouter	*to listen*	j'écoute	*I listen*
habiter	*to live*	j'habite	*I live*
jouer	*to play*	je joue	*I play*
manger	*to eat*	je mange	*I eat*
parler	*to speak*	je parle	*I speak*
porter	*to wear*	je porte	*I wear*
regarder	*to watch*	je regarde	*I watch*
travailler	*to work*	je travaille	*I work*

Note: look at *aimer, écouter, habiter – je* is shortened to *j'* before a vowel or an *h*.

Je + aime = j'aime

EXERCICE 1   Use the table on page 43 to help you say these things in French.

1 I play   5 I like   9 I eat

2 I watch   6 I speak   10 I dance

3 I listen   7 I work

4 I live   8 I wear

EXERCICE 2   Now can you give the 'je' form of these new verbs, following the same pattern? Then say what they mean in English.

1 décider (*to decide*)   3 déjeuner (*to have*   7 penser (*to think*)

     Example: je décide   *lunch*)   8 rentrer (*to return*)

     = I decide   4 entrer (*to go in*)   9 visiter (*to visit*)

2 arriver (*to arrive*)   5 marcher (*to walk*)   10 voyager (*to travel*)

                        6 montrer (*to show*)

EXERCICE 3   Complete each sentence: use the verb in brackets and put it into the 'je' form.

1 Je … un cadeau à mon copain.   6 J' … à la maison. (arriver)

   (donner)   7 Je … la porte. (fermer)

2 Je … à la piscine. (nager)   8 J' … des amis. (inviter)

3 Je … ma chambre. (ranger)   9 Je … l'escalier. (monter)

4 Je … la voiture. (laver)   10 Je … mes affaires. (chercher)

5 Je … une chanson. (chanter)

Talking to 'you' – *tu*

If you are talking to another young person or someone you know well, you use the 'tu' form or 'second person singular'. For **-er** verbs you add **-es** to the stem.

The 'tu' form is often used to ask a question. You can change a statement into a question by just adding a question mark when writing or raising your voice at the end when speaking. In English you might ask either 'Do you listen …?' or 'Are you listening?', but the French doesn't change – *Tu écoutes?*

statement		question	
tu aimes	*you like*	Tu aimes …?	*Do you like …?*
tu danses	*you dance*	Tu danses …?	*Do you dance …?*
tu écoutes	*you listen*	Tu écoutes …?	*Do you listen …?*
tu habites	*you live*	Tu habites …?	*Do you live …?*
tu joues	*you play*	Tu joues …?	*Do you play …?*
tu laves	*you wash*	Tu laves …?	*Do you wash …?*
tu manges	*you eat*	Tu manges …?	*Do you eat …?*
tu parles	*you speak*	Tu parles …?	*Do you speak …?*
tu regardes	*you watch*	Tu regardes …?	*Do you watch …?*
tu travailles	*you work*	Tu travailles …?	*Do you work …?*

Remember that in French, the **s** at the end of a word is not sounded, so the 'tu' form usually sounds the same as the 'je' form.

EXERCICE 4 Write out how you would say these in French. Use the box on page 44 to help you.

1 you dance
2 you eat
3 you like
4 you listen
5 you live
6 you watch
7 you speak
8 you wash
9 Are you playing?
10 Are you working?

EXERCICE 5 Now can you give the 'tu' form of these verbs?

1 penser (*to think*)
Example: tu penses
2 donner (*to give*)
3 inviter (*to invite*)
4 voyager (*to travel*)
5 marcher (*to walk*)
6 ranger (*to tidy up*)
7 fermer (*to close*)
8 monter (*to go up*)
9 chanter (*to sing*)
10 trouver (*to find*)

EXERCICE 6 How would you ask your friend at what time they are doing these things? Just add the 'tu' form of the verb in brackets to complete the questions.

1 Tu … à quelle heure? (arriver)
2 Tu … à quelle heure? (manger)
3 Tu … à quelle heure? (rentrer)
4 Tu … au foot à quelle heure? (jouer)
5 Tu … à quelle heure? (nager)
6 Tu … la télé à quelle heure? (regarder)
7 Tu … la voiture à quelle heure? (laver)
8 Tu … ta chambre à quelle heure? (ranger)
9 Tu … à la tour Eiffel à quelle heure? (monter)
10 Tu … la porte à quelle heure? (fermer)

Another way of asking a question in French is to swap round the *tu* and the verb, and join them with a hyphen:

Tu manges des bananes? Manges-tu des bananes? *Do you eat bananas?*

Tu voyages en train? Voyages-tu en train? *Are you travelling by train?*

EXERCICE 7 Now change these questions in the same way:

1 Tu manges des frites?
2 Tu arrives à la gare?
3 Tu joues au tennis?
4 Tu ranges ta chambre?
5 Tu cherches tes affaires?
6 Tu montes à la tour Eiffel?

Talking about someone else – *il/elle*

If you are talking about someone else, in English, you use the 'he/she' form, or 'third person singular'. In French, this is the 'il/elle' form and for **-er** verbs you add **-e** to the stem.

Marie joue	*Marie plays*	il écoute	*he listens*
il joue	*he plays*	elle habite	*she lives*
elle travaille	*she works*	Alain aime	*Alain likes*
il regarde	*he watches*	le chien mange	*the dog is eating*

EXERCICE 8 How would you say the following in French, using the verb in brackets?

1 she likes (aimer)
  Example: elle aime
2 he listens (écouter)
3 he watches (regarder)

4 she lives (habiter)
5 she speaks (parler)
6 he dances (danser)
7 she plays (jouer)

8 he works (travailler)
9 John eats (manger)
10 Maureen wears (porter)

EXERCICE 9 What are Juliette and Julien doing this week? Fill the gap in each sentence, using the verb in brackets in the 'il/elle' form.

1 Juliette … Paris. (visiter)
2 Elle … la journée au Louvre. (passer)
3 Elle … des tableaux. (regarder)
4 Elle … dans un restaurant. (manger)
5 Elle … à neuf heures du soir. (rentrer)

6 Julien … sa chambre. (ranger)
7 Il … la voiture de son père. (laver)
8 Il … au football. (jouer)
9 Il … son ballon de foot. (chercher)
10 Il … ses copains chez lui. (inviter)

Talking about us: we – *nous*

If you are talking about yourself and someone else you use the 'we' form, or 'first person plural'. In French, this is the 'nous' form. For **-er** verbs, you add **-ons** to the stem. Remember, you find the stem by removing the infinitive ending, for example, *regarder* → *regard-*

nous regardons	*we watch*	nous aimons	*we like*
nous écoutons	*we listen*	nous parlons	*we speak*
nous habitons	*we live*		

EXERCICE 10 How would you say these in French, using the verb in brackets?

1 we play (jouer)
2 we like (aimer)
3 we listen (écouter)
4 we live (habiter)
5 we dance (danser)

6 we speak (parler)
7 we wash (laver)
8 we watch (regarder)
9 we wear (porter)
10 we work (travailler)

Verbs which end in **-ger** add an **e** before the ending, to keep the **g** sound soft.

manger → nous mang**eons** (*we eat*)
nager → nous nag**eons** (*we swim*)

Verbs which end in **-cer** add a cedilla to the **c** – **ç** – to keep its soft sound.

commencer → nous commen**çons** (*we begin*)

EXERCICE 11 Now complete these sentences using the 'nous' form of the verb at the end.

1 Nous … du collège. (rentrer)
2 Nous … pendant le week-end. (travailler)
3 Nous … à la maison. (aider)
4 Nous … la vaisselle. (laver)
5 Nous … le repas. (préparer)

6 Nous … les bananes. (manger)
7 Nous … de la musique. (écouter)
8 Nous … une chanson. (chanter)
9 Nous … la télévision. (regarder)
10 Nous … aux échecs. (jouer)

Talking to 'you' – *vous*

In English, we have only one word for 'you', whether we are talking to one or more people. In French, there are two words:

– *tu* if you are talking to one person in an informal situation,

– *vous* if you are talking to more than one person.
Vous is also known as the polite form, because you also use it when talking to someone older than yourself or someone that you don't know.

See pages 15–16 for more about *tu* and *vous*.

For **-er** verbs, the 'vous' form (or 'second person plural') is made by adding **-ez** to the stem of the infinitive.

vous regardez	*you watch*	vous aimez	*you like*
vous écoutez	*you listen*	vous parlez	*you speak*
vous habitez	*you live*	vous mangez	*you eat*

EXERCICE 12 How would you say these in French?

1 you like (aimer)
2 you eat (manger)
3 you live (habiter)
4 you speak (parler)
5 you play (jouer)

6 you listen (écouter)
7 you watch (regarder)
8 you look for (chercher)
9 you find (trouver)
10 you invite (inviter)

The 'vous' form, like the 'tu' form, is often used to ask questions. You can turn a statement into a question by raising your voice at the end of it or by inverting (swapping over) the *vous* and the verb.

EXERCICE 13 Make each statement into two kinds of questions.

1 Vous parlez anglais. *Example: Vous parlez anglais? Parlez-vous anglais?*
2 Vous aimez danser.
3 Vous écoutez du jazz.
4 Vous regardez souvent la télé.
5 Vous mangez de la viande.
6 Vous chantez bien.

Talking about them: they – *ils/elles*

To talk about more than one person in English, you use 'they' or the 'third person plural'.

In English, we have only one word for 'they'. French has two words: *ils* and *elles*. If the people you are talking about are all male, or a mix of male and female, you use *ils*. If they are all female, you use *elles*.

For **-er** verbs, the 'ils/elles' form is made by adding **-ent** to the stem of the verb.

ils regardent	*they watch*	elles bavardent	*they chat*
elles écoutent	*they listen*	ils mangent	*they eat*
ils rentrent	*they go home*		

EXERCICE 14 Give the right form of the verb in brackets. Remember, find the stem and add **-ent**.

1 ils (bavarder)
2 elles (écouter)
3 ils (rentrer)
4 elles (rester)

5 ils (pousser)
6 elles (tirer)
7 ils (chercher)
8 elles (trouver)

9 les filles (regarder)
10 les garçons (jouer)

EXERCICE 15 Can you complete these sentences by adding the right form of the verb?

1 Ils … la vaisselle. (laver)

2 Elles … la chambre. (ranger)

3 Corinne et sa sœur … la télé. (regarder)

4 Paul et Simon … aux cartes. (jouer)

5 Les garçons … des CD. (écouter)

6 Les parents de Corinne … le samedi. (travailler)

7 M. et Mme Hibert … anglais. (parler)

8 Les élèves … des sweat-shirts bleus. (porter)

9 Caroline et Monique … des frites. (manger)

10 Paul et sa sœur … les animaux. (aimer)

> Don't forget that if 'they' include males and females then you should use *ils* for the whole group, even if there's only one male!

Voici mes copains. Ils sont sympathiques, non?

EXERCICE 16 Look back over pages 43–49 and at the table of endings on page 43. Then see how much you can remember about **-er** verbs by putting these infinitives into the correct form for the person given. What does each one mean?

1 je (danser) *Example: je danse = I dance (or I'm dancing)*

2 ils (parler)

3 tu (ranger)

4 nous (regarder)

5 vous (jouer)

6 elles (laver)

7 il (travailler)

8 vous (aimer)

9 nous (habiter)

10 ils (porter)

EXERCICE 17 Now complete the sentences by adding the right form of the verb given.

1 Je … un jean. (porter)

2 Paul et Jean … de la glace. (manger)

3 Mélanie … français. (parler)

4 Tu … à Paris. (habiter)

5 Vous … la vaisselle. (laver)

6 Monique … sa chambre. (ranger)

7 Céline et moi … de la musique. (écouter)

8 Son père … la télé. (regarder)

9 Sa mère … dans un bureau. (travailler)

10 Son frère … au foot. (jouer)

4.2 The present tense: -ir and -re verbs

EXERCICE 1 Look back at page 42 to remind yourself about the three groups of verbs in French and about what an 'infinitive' and a 'stem' are.

Then sort these verbs into **-ir** and **-re** verbs: remember to look at the last two letters. Make two lists: <u>-ir verbs</u>   <u>-re verbs</u>

choisir écrire finir grossir sentir
partir répondre réussir sortir vendre

The present tense: -ir verbs

There are two different patterns for **-ir** verbs. Some like *finir, choisir, réussir,* add **-iss** in the 'nous', 'vous' and 'ils/elles' forms. Others, like *dormir, partir, sortir,* lose the last letter of the stem in the 'je', 'tu' and 'il/elle' forms. For both patterns, you then add endings.

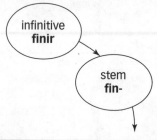

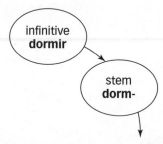

je fin**is**	*I finish*
tu fin**is**	*you finish*
il/elle fin**it**	*he/she/it finishes*
nous fin**issons**	*we finish*
vous fin**issez**	*you finish*
ils/elles fin**issent**	*they finish*

je dor**s**	*I sleep*
tu dor**s**	*you sleep*
il/elle dor**t**	*he/she/it sleeps*
nous dorm**ons**	*we sleep*
vous dorm**ez**	*you sleep*
ls/elles dorm**ent**	*they sleep*

EXERCICE 2 See if you can give the right form of the verb in brackets. These verbs all follow the pattern of *finir*, adding **-iss** in the plural.

1 je (finir)   **3** tu (remplir)   **5** elles (choisir)
2 vous (réussir)   **4** il (grossir)   **6** nous (finir)

EXERCICE 3 See if you can give the right form of the verb in brackets. These verbs follow the pattern of *dormir*.

1 ils (partir)   **3** tu (sortir)   **5** elle (repartir)
2 nous (dormir)   **4** je (sentir)   **6** il (partir)

EXERCICE 4 Now complete these sentences and translate them into English.

1 Ils … l'exercice. (finir)
2 Nous … de la maison. (sortir)
3 Je … le formulaire. (remplir)
4 Vous … de bonne heure. (sortir)
5 Elle … une nouvelle robe. (choisir)

6 Tu … à compléter l'exercice? (réussir)
7 Le bébé … (dormir)
8 Il … son repas. (finir)
9 Les filles … beaucoup. (sortir)
10 Mes chats … (grossir)

The present tense: -re verbs

The third group of verbs are those that end in **-re**. To form the present tense you need the stem first, then add endings:

je vend**s**	*I sell*
tu vend**s**	*you sell*
il/elle vend	*he/she/it sells*
nous vend**ons**	*we sell*
vous vend**ez**	*you sell*
ils/elles vend**ent**	*they sell*

EXERCICE 5 Complete the sentences by changing each infinitive to the present tense of the verb.

1 Je … (descendre) l'escalier.
2 Ils … (vendre) leur maison.
3 Nous … (attendre) les autres.
4 Vous … (répondre) aux questions.
5 Tu … (attendre) ton amie?
6 Chantal … (répondre) à la question.

7 Pascal … (vendre) son vélo.
8 Les copains … (attendre) leurs copines.
9 Je … (descendre) la rue.
10 Le négociant … (vendre) les fruits et les légumes.

To help you learn the present tense, it's worth noticing that for **-er**, **-ir** and **-re** verbs, the endings for 'nous', 'vous' and 'ils/elles' are always the same:

■ nous **-ons**
■ vous **-ez**
■ ils/elles **-ent**

4.3 The present tense: irregular verbs

Irregular verbs don't fit into the three main groups (see page 42) but follow their own patterns. Here are nine very useful ones that you should learn.

Avoir (to have) and *être* (to be) are the most commonly used verbs. They are also used to form other tenses so once you've learnt them you'll be able to say a lot more in French.

avoir *to have*			
j'ai	*I have*	nous avons	*we have*
tu as	*you have*	vous avez	*you have*
il/elle a	*he/she/it has*	ils/elles ont	*they have*

EXERCICE 1 Complete these sentences by adding the right part of the present tense of *avoir*.

1 J' … un frère.

2 Il … dix ans.

3 Nous … un grand jardin.

4 Mes parents … une vieille voiture.

5 Mon frère … un chat.

6 Tu … un animal à la maison?

7 J' … un chien.

8 Paul et Louise … un oiseau.

9 Mon copain … un petit frère.

10 Quel âge … –vous?

être *to be*			
je suis	*I am*	nous sommes	*we are*
tu es	*you are*	vous êtes	*you are*
il/elle est	*he/she/it is*	ils/elles sont	*they are*

EXERCICE 2 Fill the gap with the correct part of the present tense of *être*.

1 Mon père … français.

2 Je … britannique.

3 Tu … française?

4 Ils … bavards.

5 Mon frère … grand.

6 Ma sœur … petite.

7 Les enfants … contents.

8 Nous … fatigués.

9 Vous … fatigué?

10 Mes parents … fatigués.

EXERCICE 3 This time you have to decide whether it's *avoir* or *être* and which part to use!

1 Je … français.

2 J' … douze ans.

3 Mon copain … treize ans.

4 Il … grand et marrant.

5 Nous … fanas de foot.

6 Il y … un match de foot ce soir.

7 … –vous des billets pour le match?

8 Ma copine … douze ans comme moi.

9 Elle … grande et branchée.

10 … –tu une copine?

There is a group of verbs which have regular **-er** endings but which have an irregular stem. The 'nous' and 'vous' forms have the same stem as the infinitive.

payer *to pay*			
je paie	*I pay*	nous payons	*we pay*
tu paies	*you pay*	vous payez	*you pay*
il/elle paie	*he/she/it pays*	ils/elles paient	*they pay*

Other verbs that follow the same pattern as *payer* include: *envoyer* (to send), *essayer* (to try), *nettoyer* (to clean).

EXERCICE 4 Complete these sentences with the correct part of the verb in brackets.

1 J' … la lettre. (envoyer)

2 Il … l'addition. (payer)

3 Vous … la cuisine. (nettoyer)

4 Nous … de monter la colline. (essayer)

5 Elles … des cadeaux aux enfants. (envoyer)

acheter *to buy*			
j'achète	*I buy*	nous achetons	*we buy*
tu achètes	*you buy*	vous achetez	*you buy*
il/elle achète	*he/she/it buys*	ils/elles achètent	*they buy*

EXERCICE 5 Complete these sentences with the correct part of the verb *acheter*.

1 Ma mère … des légumes.

2 J'… des fruits.

3 Où …-tu du pain?

4 Nous … du fromage au marché.

5 Mes frères … des bonbons.

6 Qu'est-ce que vous … ?

Many **-re** verbs are irregular and you will find the most useful ones in the table on pages 95–96. There is a group of verbs which have regular **-re** endings but which have an irregular stem in the 'nous', 'vous' and 'ils/elles' forms.

prendre *to take*			
je prends	*I take*	nous prenons	*we take*
tu prends	*you take*	vous prenez	*you take*
il/elle prend	*he/she/it takes*	ils/elles prennent	*they take*

Other verbs that follow the same pattern as *prendre* include: *apprendre* (to learn), *comprendre* (to understand).

EXERCICE 6 Complete these sentences with the correct part of the verb in brackets.

1 Je … le café. (prendre)

2 Vous … du sucre? (prendre)

3 Mon copain … l'allemand. (apprendre)

4 Les filles … l'espagnol. (apprendre)

5 Tu … l'italien? (comprendre)

6 Mes parents ne … pas. (comprendre)

aller *to go*			
je vais	*I go*	nous allons	*we go*
tu vas	*you go*	vous allez	*you go*
il/elle va	*he/she/it goes*	ils/elles vont	*they go*

EXERCICE 7 Give the right form of the verb *aller* to complete each sentence.

1 Je … au cinéma.

2 … –vous au cinéma avec lui?

3 Nous … en ville.

4 Maurice … en ville avec nous.

5 Les filles … en ville aussi.

6 Où … –tu?

7 Tu … au marché?

8 Ils … au match de foot.

9 Mes parents ne … pas en ville.

10 Ma mère … au supermarché.

faire *to do/to make*			
je fais	*I do*	nous faisons	*we do*
tu fais	*you do*	vous faites	*you do*
il/elle fait	*he/she/it does*	ils/elles font	*they do*

EXERCICE 8 Add part of the present tense of *faire* to complete each sentence.

1 Mon frère … ses devoirs.

2 Que … –tu?

3 Moi aussi, je … mes devoirs.

4 Mes parents … du footing.

5 Je ne … pas de footing.

6 … –vous du footing?

7 Nicolas … du bricolage.

8 Denis et moi, nous … de la cuisine.

9 Nous … un gâteau.

10 Il … beau aujourd'hui.

EXERCICE 9 Now choose whether you need part of *aller* or *faire* to complete each sentence.

1 Pendant les vacances, nous … au bord de la mer.

2 Nous … de la planche à voile.

3 Mes parents … de la voile.

4 Mon frère aîné … du ski nautique.

5 Ma sœur … de l'équitation.

6 Le matin, je … à la boulangerie.

7 Maman … au marché pour faire les achats.

8 Mon père … au tabac pour chercher son journal.

9 Le soir, mes parents … au bar.

10 Où …–tu? Que … –tu?

venir *to come*			
je viens	*I come*	nous venons	*we come*
tu viens	*you come*	vous venez	*you come*
il/elle vient	*he/she/it comes*	ils/elles viennent	*they come*

Notice that the stem changes: *venir → vien-*

Other verbs that end in -venir, such as devenir (to become) and revenir (to come back), behave in the same way: *je deviens*, *je reviens*.

EXERCICE 10 Can you complete these sentences by adding part of the present tense of *venir*?

1 Je … au collège à vélo.

2 Ma sœur … au cinéma avec nous.

3 Nous allons et … toute la journée.

4 Mon copain … d'Afrique.

5 Ses parents … du Maroc.

6 D'où … –tu?

7 Les filles … du sud.

8 Les garçons … du nord.

9 Vous … du nord aussi?

10 Nous … de l'ouest.

ouvrir *to open*			
j'ouvre	*I open*	nous ouvrons	*we open*
tu ouvres	*you open*	vous ouvrez	*you open*
il/elle ouvre	*he/she/it opens*	ils/elles ouvrent	*they open*

Other verbs ending in -rir follow the same pattern as ouvrir: couvrir (to cover), découvrir (to discover), offrir (to offer/to give), souffrir (to suffer).

EXERCICE 11 Complete the sentences with the correct part of the verb in brackets. Can you say what they mean?

1 Il … et ferme la porte. (ouvrir)

2 Ils … beaucoup à cause de la chaleur. (souffrir)

3 … la casserole et mettez–la au four. (couvrir)

4 Ils … la vérité. (découvrir)

5 La neige … la terre. (couvrir)

6 Tu … un cadeau à Jacques pour son anniversaire? (offrir)

4.4 The present tense: reflexive verbs

There is a separate category of verbs in French called 'reflexive verbs'. Reflexive verbs always have a reflexive pronoun between the subject and the verb:

Je **me** lave. Il **s'**appelle Jean.

The equivalent in English often includes words like 'myself', 'himself', 'themselves', but very often there is a better way to translate the phrase.

For example: Je me lave = I wash myself = I get washed

Il s'appelle Jean = He calls himself John = He's called John

These are the reflexive pronouns:

me/m'	myself	nous	ourselves
te/t'	yourself	vous	yourselves
se/s'	himself/herself	se/s'	themselves

se laver   to get washed

je me lave	I get washed	nous nous lavons	we get washed
tu te laves	you get washed	vous vous lavez	you get washed
il/elle se lave	he/she gets washed	ils/elles se lavent	they get washed

useful reflexive verbs

se coucher	to go to bed	se doucher	to have a shower
se lever	to get up	s'appeler	to be called
se réveiller	to wake up	s'habiller	to get dressed

EXERCICE 1   Give the right form of these verbs:

1 Tu ...? (s'habiller)

Example: Tu t'habilles?

2 Je ... (se laver)

3 Ils ... (se doucher)

4 Nathalie et Corinne ... (s'habiller)

5 Thomas ... (se coucher)

6 Vous ... à quelle heure? (se coucher)

7 Nous ... (s'habiller)

8 Elle ... (se réveiller)

EXERCICE 2   How would you translate these into French?

1 He gets washed.

2 She gets washed.

3 Are you going to bed? (tu)

4 We go to bed at nine o'clock.

5 Are you getting dressed? (vous)

6 I'm having a shower.

7 I wake up at eight o'clock.

8 You wake up. (tu)

4.5 Imperatives

The 'imperative' is what you use when you are telling someone to do something or giving instructions: 'Please sit down.' 'Open your books.' 'Turn left.'

The imperative is simply the 'you' part of the verb. In French, you have to decide whether to use the 'tu' form or the 'vous' form. Remember that you use the 'tu' form when speaking to someone you know well or someone younger than you. You use the 'vous' form when speaking to an older person or someone you don't know, and when you are speaking to more than one person.

The imperative is the same as the 'tu' or the 'vous' form of the present tense (without the *tu/vous*). For **-er** verbs you drop the final **-s** for the 'tu' form:

> tu regardes → **Regarde** le livre.

Look at the examples in the table. Which ones do you recognise?

'tu' form	'vous' form	translation
Ouvre le livre.	Ouvrez le livre.	*Open the book*.
Regarde page 23.	Regardez page 23.	*Look at page 23*.
Lis l'exercice.	Lisez l'exercice.	*Read the text*.
Ecoute la bande.	Ecoutez la bande.	*Listen to the tape*.
Réponds à la question.	Répondez à la question.	*Answer the question*.
Fais tes devoirs.	Faites vos devoirs.	*Do your homework*.
Traverse la rue.	Traversez la rue.	*Cross the road*.
Tourne à gauche.	Tournez à gauche.	*Turn left*.
Vas-y!	Allez-y!	*Go on!*
Tais-toi.*	Taisez-vous.*	*Be quiet*. (se taire)
Assieds-toi.*	Asseyez-vous.*	*Sit down*. (s'asseoir)
Dépêche-toi.*	Dépêchez-vous.*	*Hurry up*. (se dépêcher)

* The last three are reflexive verbs, so they need an extra pronoun, *-toi* or *-vous*, directly after the imperative.

EXERCICE 1 Give these instructions to someone, using the 'tu' form.

1 (tourner) à gauche.
   Example: Tourne à gauche.

2 (marcher) vite.

3 (prendre) la première rue à gauche!

4 (attendre) le feu vert.

5 (regarder) à droite et à gauche.

6 (traverser) la rue.

7 (monter) l'escalier.

8 (descendre) la rue.

9 (aller) –y!

10 (arrêter)!

EXERCICE 2 Here are some instructions for a recipe for *Quiche à l'oignon*. Put them in the 'tu' form to tell a friend how to make it.

1 (préchauffer) le four.

2 (couper) l'oignon en dés.

3 (fouetter) les œufs.

4 (ajouter) du lait.

5 (mélanger) bien.

6 (beurrer) un moule.

7 (étaler) la pâte dans le moule.

8 (verser) les œufs et l'oignon dans le moule.

9 (ajouter) du fromage râpé.

10 (faire) cuire pendant 40 minutes.

EXERCICE 3 How would you tell someone to do these things? Use the 'vous' form.

1 (écouter) la radio

2 (regarder) la télé

3 (manger) les légumes

4 (boire) de l'eau

5 (fermer) la porte

6 (ouvrir) la fenêtre

7 (ranger) vos affaires

8 (parler) plus lentement

9 (venir) ici

10 (acheter) un billet

EXERCICE 4 Change the infinitives to imperatives to tell some visitors the way to the station. Use the 'vous' form.

1 (sortir) d'ici.

2 (prendre) la deuxième rue à droite.

3 (traverser) la place.

4 (tourner) à gauche.

5 (aller) tout droit.

6 (trouver) l'arrêt de bus.

7 (attendre) le bus.

8 (monter) dans le bus.

9 (composter) votre billet.

10 (descendre) devant la gare.

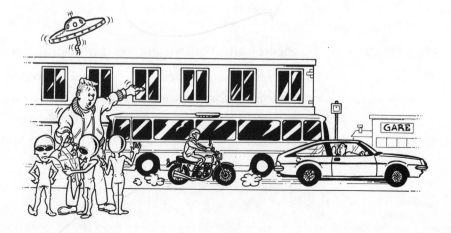

4.6 The perfect tense

When we talk about something we've done or something that has happened, we use a past tense: I <u>played</u> tennis on Saturday. We <u>watched</u> a film. He <u>has eaten</u> all the biscuits.

In French, there are two main past tenses, the 'perfect' and the 'imperfect'. The one you will use most often is the perfect tense. You use the perfect tense to talk about something that happened on a particular occasion in the past. (The imperfect is explained on pages 67–68).

In English, we can talk about the past using the verb 'to have' and a past participle. For example: 'He has eaten all the biscuits.' We can also say 'He ate all the biscuits.'

The perfect tense in French is formed using the present tense of *avoir* (to have) and a past participle: **Il a mangé** tous les petits gâteaux.

Il a mangé is the equivalent of both 'He has eaten' and 'He ate'. In the same way, *j'ai joué* means both 'I have played' and 'I played'.

To form the perfect tense you need to know two things:

- **how to form the past participle**

English past participles often end in **-ed**: played, watched, danced.

In French **-er**, **-ir** and **-re** verbs form their past participles in different ways:

	-er verbs	**-ir** verbs	**-re** verbs
take off:	**-er**	**-ir**	**-re**
and add:	**-é**	**-i**	**-u**
example:	parler → parlé	dormir → dormi	répondre → répondu

Using those rules, what would the past participles of these verbs be?

jouer   manger   finir   vendre   écouter

perdre   choisir   attendre   visiter   inviter

- **the present tense of** *avoir*

avoir *to have*

j'ai	I have
tu as	you have
il a	he/it has
elle a	she/it has
nous avons	we have
vous avez	you have
ils ont	they have
elles ont	they have

Avoir is called an 'auxiliary' (= helpful) verb because it 'helps' form the perfect tense.

To form the perfect tense you put together the right part of *avoir* and the past participle of the verb you are using. Can you spot those two components in these examples?

J'ai mangé. *I have eaten. / I ate.*

Tu as dormi où? *Where did you sleep?*

Il a vendu sa maison. *He has sold his house. / He sold his house.*

Nous avons dansé. *We have danced. / We danced.*

Vous avez mangé le gâteau. *You have eaten the cake. / You ate the cake.*

Ils ont fini leurs devoirs. *They have finished their homework.*

EXERCICE 1 Who watched the film? Complete these sentences by adding the right part of *avoir*.

1 Nous … regardé le film.

2 J' … regardé le film.

3 Il … regardé le film.

4 Tu … regardé le film?

5 Ils … regardé le film.

6 Elle … regardé le film.

7 Elles n' … pas regardé le film.

8 Vous … regardé le film?

9 Julie … regardé le film.

10 Mes parents n' … pas regardé le film.

Did you notice that sentences 7 and 10 are negative? (They <u>didn't</u> watch the film.) More about how to use negatives with the perfect tense on page 74.

EXERCICE 2 Add the right part of *avoir* to complete these sentences:

1 J' … joué au football hier soir.

2 Nous … mangé au McDo.

3 Il … fini ses devoirs.

4 Elle … vendu sa bicyclette.

5 Vous … fini?

6 Maurice … perdu son sac.

7 J' … acheté un cadeau.

8 Ils … attendu devant le cinéma.

9 Mes parents … mangé chez ma grand-mère.

10 Charlotte … invité ses copains à sa boum.

EXERCICE 3 Complete these sentences by adding the right form of *avoir* and the past participle of the verb in brackets.

1 Maman … (préparer) le repas.

2 Nadine … (débarrasser) la table.

3 Son père … (laver) la vaisselle.

4 Son frère … (ranger) sa chambre.

5 Elle … (inviter) ses copains.

6 J' … (téléphoner) à mon copain.

7 Ils … (écouter) de la musique.

8 Vous … (jouer) aux cartes?

9 Ma mère … (dormir) devant la télé.

10 Nous … (regarder) la télé.

Irregular past participles

Some **-ir** and **-re** verbs have irregular past participles, in other words, they don't simply end in **-i** or **-u**. Here are some of the most common ones. They are easy to learn as they follow patterns.

ending in -u		
avoir	eu	J'ai eu une surprise. *I had a surprise.*
boire	bu	Nous avons bu du vin. *We drank some wine.*
devoir	dû	Il a dû rentrer. *He had to go home.*
lire	lu	Il a lu le livre. *He has read the book.*
recevoir	reçu	Elle a reçu une bonne note. *She received a good mark.*
voir	vu	Il a vu le journal. *He has seen/saw the newspaper.*

EXERCICE 4   Complete these sentences by adding the past participle of the verb in brackets.

1 Ils ont … (boire) du vin.

2 J'ai … (lire) le journal.

3 Martine a … (recevoir) une lettre.

4 M. Bertrand a … (avoir) un accident.

5 Nous avons … (voir) le film.

6 J'ai … (devoir) ranger ma chambre.

EXERCICE 5   Now tell the story of Benoît's new bike. Copy out the sentences, changing each infinitive in brackets into a past participle. Then read out the whole story. Beware: the verbs are not all irregular!

> Benoît a (recevoir) de l'argent pour son anniversaire. Il a (voir) une petite annonce dans un journal. Il a (acheter) la bicyclette. Il a (laisser) sa nouvelle bicyclette deux minutes devant la maison. Quelqu'un a (voler) sa bicyclette. Quel désastre!

EXERCICE 6   This time see if you can add the right form of *avoir* as well as the past participle. (Not all the verbs are irregular.)

1 J' … … de l'argent pour mon anniversaire. (recevoir)

2 Tu … … les chansons de Vanessa Paradis. (écouter)

3 J' … … mon copain Gilles au McDo. (inviter)

4 Nous … … des Big Mac. (manger)

5 Il … … un milk-shake. (boire)

6 J' … … un coca. (boire)

7 Mes copains … … une BD pour moi. (acheter)

8 Nous … … le film Frankenstein. (voir)

9 Vous … … le film? (voir)

10 J' … … le livre. (lire)

ending in -s		
prendre	pris	Elle a pris son parapluie. *She took her umbrella.*
apprendre	appris	Elle a appris la leçon. *She learnt the lesson.*
comprendre	compris	J'ai compris. *I understood.*
mettre	mis	Il a mis son imperméable. *He put on his raincoat.*

ending in -t		
faire	fait	J'ai fait mes devoirs. *I did my homework.*
dire	dit	Il m'a dit bonjour. *He said hello to me.*
écrire	écrit	Elle a écrit une lettre. *She wrote a letter.*

EXERCICE 7 Use the past participle of the verb in brackets to complete these sentences. Then translate them.

1 Nous avons … l'autobus. (prendre)
2 Vous avez … vos devoirs? (faire)
3 J'ai … une lettre. (écrire)
4 Nous avons … les verbes. (apprendre)
5 Ma sœur a … la table. (mettre)
6 Mon frère n'a rien … (comprendre)
7 Il a … du vélo. (faire)
8 Il m'a … de venir demain. (dire)

EXERCICE 8 Fill the gap in each sentence with the perfect tense of the verb in brackets. Without looking back at the lists above, see how many of these irregular past participles you can remember. Then use the lists to check.

1 Marc … … (avoir) une glace au citron.
2 Stéphanie … … (voir) son petit copain.
3 Nous … … (faire) nos devoirs.
4 J' … … (recevoir) une lettre.
5 Ils … … (boire) de l'eau.
6 Vous … … (prendre) le bus?
7 Paul … … (écrire) la lettre.
8 Il … … (dire) 'Salut'.
9 Tu … … (comprendre)?
10 Elles … … (lire) le livre.

The perfect tense: verbs which take *être*

As you saw on page 59, the perfect tense is usually formed from the present tense of *avoir* and a past participle: *J'ai regardé* = 'I have seen' or 'I saw'.

However, some verbs use the present tense of *être* instead of *avoir*: *Je suis arrivé* = 'I have arrived' or 'I arrived'.

Just as with *avoir*, the present tense of *être* is combined with a past participle to make the perfect tense. Read these examples, and see that each one contains part of the present tense of *être* and a past participle.

Je **suis allé** en France.	*I went/I've been to France.*
Tu **es allé** au cinéma?	*Did you go to the cinema?*
Il **est venu** chez nous.	*He came to our house.*
Elle **est venue** chez nous aussi.	*She came to our house too.*
Nous **sommes restés** une semaine.	*We stayed for a week.*
Vous **êtes entré** dans le musée?	*Did you go into the museum?*
Ils **sont partis** hier.	*They left yesterday.*
Elles **sont descendues** à Dijon.	*They got out at Dijon.*

EXERCICE 9   Use the right part of *être* to complete these sentences.

1 Je … allé au collège.

2 Nous … allées en ville.

3 Mes copains … allés au cinéma.

4 Mon père … allé au travail.

5 Ma mère … allée au supermarché.

6 Vous … allés en ville?

7 Mes copines … allées à la piscine.

8 Sophie, où … -tu allée?

9 Où …-vous allés?

10 Nous ne … pas allés à la piscine.

Here is a list of verbs which take *être* rather than *avoir* in the perfect tense. An easy way to remember them is to think of them as verbs of motion (or coming and going verbs). Try learning them in pairs.

aller	*to go*	↔	venir	*to come*
arriver	*to arrive*	↔	partir	*to leave*
entrer	*to go in*	↔	sortir	*to go out*
monter	*to go up*	↔	descendre	*to go down*
rester	*to stay*	↔	tomber	*to fall*
naître	*to be born*	↔	mourir	*to die*

All their past participles are regular, except *naître → né*, *mourir → mort* and *venir → venu*.

So *arriver → arrivé*, *sortir → sorti*, *descendre → descendu* (see page 59).

Reflexive verbs also take *être* in the perfect tense. So do verbs made up of the ones listed above, such as *repartir*, *rentrer*, *ressortir*.

Making the past participle agree

You have probably noticed that with *être* the past participle often has an extra ending. (If you didn't notice, look back at exercise 9!) It depends on who or what the verbs refers to – rather like endings on adjectives. Look at two examples:

- Martine est allée au cinéma.
  The verb refers to *Martine*, a girl, so the past participle has an extra **-e**.

- Le train est parti.
  Le train is a masculine noun, so there is no change to the past participle.

It's easy with *il* and *elle*, but remember that you also need to check for masculine and feminine endings whenever you use *je*, *tu*, *nous* and *vous*.

Les vacances

EXERCICE 10 Add the past participle to these sentences. Remember to add the **-e** ending when it refers to a girl or feminine object. ((*f*) means feminine and (*m*) means masculine.) Then translate them into English.

1 Jeanne est … en ville. (aller)

2 Il est … de la maison à neuf heures vingt. (sortir)

3 Le bus est … à neuf heures et demie. (partir)

4 Il est … à dix heures. (arriver)

5 Je (*f*) suis … de l'autobus devant le cinéma. (descendre)

6 Elle est … dans l'hôpital. (entrer)

7 Tu (*m*) es … à quelle heure? (venir)

8 Il est … tout de suite. (monter)

9 Je (*m*) suis … dans l'escalier. (tomber)

10 Elle est … à l'hôpital. (rester)

When you're talking about more than one person or thing, you need to add **-s** to the past participle. Add a feminine plural ending, **-es**, if the group is all feminine. Look at some examples:

- Nous sommes allées en ville.

  This must be a group of women or girls as the past participle ends in **-es**. If there were any men or boys in the group, you would have to use *allés* instead.

- Vous êtes arrivées en retard. Vous êtes arrivés en retard.

  The first group are all female, the second group are all male or mixed.

- Ils sont partis. Elles sont parties.

  Ils and *elles* are easy to use, since *ils* always needs just **-s** added to the past participle, *elles* needs **-es**. You have to work it out if you're talking about *les élèves, les chats, les classes*, and so on – are they masculine or feminine?

EXERCICE 11 Now try adding the past participle of the verb in brackets, with **-s** or **-es** as necessary. Some sentences use (*fpl*) to indicate feminine plural and (*mpl*) for masculine plural.

1 Sandrine et ses parents sont … à Paris. (aller)

2 Ils sont … de la maison à neuf heures vingt. (sortir)

3 Vous (*fpl*) êtes … au cinéma? (aller)

4 Elles sont … à neuf heures et demie. (partir)

5 Nous (*mpl*) sommes … à dix heures. (arriver)

6 Ils sont … à la gare St-Lazare. (descendre)

7 Sandrine et son frère sont … à la tour Eiffel. (monter)

8 Vous (*mpl*) êtes … en bas. (rester)

9 Mélanie et Christine sont … pour visiter le musée du Louvre. (venir)

10 Nous (*fpl*) sommes … dans le musée. (entrer)

EXERCICE 12 The next sentences all need the past participle of *aller* to fill the gap. Make it agree with the subject – decide between *allé*, *allée*, *allés* and *allées*.

1 Ludo est … à Londres.

2 Sa copine Charlotte est … à Paris.

3 Ses parents sont … sur la côte d'Azur.

4 Ses sœurs sont … en Espagne.

5 Nous (*fpl*) sommes … en Bretagne.

6 Vous (*mpl*) êtes … en France.

7 Mes grands-parents sont … en Italie.

8 Mon copain est … en Suisse.

9 Tu es … aux Etats-Unis, Marc.

10 Et moi? Je suis … au bord de la mer!

EXERCICE 13 Fill the gap in each sentence with the past participle of the verb in brackets. Say what ending is needed, if any. Then translate the sentences into English.

1 Le train est … en retard. (arriver)

2 Mes parents sont … à sept heures. (partir)

3 Elle est … hier. (venir)

4 Le chat est … dans l'arbre. (monter)

5 Il est … de l'arbre. (tomber)

6 Les filles sont … dans le cinéma. (entrer)

7 Ma grand-mère est … en 1950. (naître)

8 Mon grand-père est … l'année dernière. (mourir)

9 Les garçons sont … (sortir)

10 Monique est … en ville. (aller)

The perfect tense: reflexive verbs

All reflexive verbs use the present tense of *être* to form the perfect tense. (See page 56 for an introduction to reflexive verbs.)

Look at the verb *se lever* (to get up) in the perfect tense.

je me suis levé(e)	*I got up*	nous nous sommes levé(e)s	*we got up*
tu t'es levé(e)	*you got up*	vous vous êtes levé(e)(s)	*you got up*
il s'est levé	*he got up*	ils se sont levés	*they got up*
elle s'est levée	*she got up*	elles se sont levées	*they got up*

Notice the reflexive pronouns – *me, t', s', nous, vous, se* – between the subject and the relevant part of *être*. Notice the word order too – *être* comes immediately before the past participle.

As with other verbs that take *être*, the past participle of reflexive verbs must agree with who has done the action. So to say that you got up this morning at 6 a.m., if you're male, you would say *Je me suis levé à six heures*. If you're female, you would say *Je me suis levée à six heures*. Both sentences sound the same but *levé* needs to be written with an extra **-e** for the feminine subject.

EXERCICE 14 When did Benjamin's family and friends get up? Use *levé, levée, levés* or *levées* to complete each sentence.

1 Ce matin, je me suis … à sept heures.

2 Mes parents se sont … à six heures.

3 Mon grand frère s'est … à sept heures et demie.

4 Ma sœur s'est … à huit heures moins le quart.

5 Mon petit frère et moi, nous nous sommes … à sept heures.

6 Céline, à quelle heure tu t'es … ?

7 Mes copines se sont … à neuf heures.

8 Mon copain s'est … à dix heures.

9 Gilles et Patrice se sont … à neuf heures et demie.

10 Et vous, à quelle heure vous vous êtes … ce matin?

Now look at these other reflexive verbs. The 'je' part of the perfect tense is given. You can work out the other parts, using *se lever* on page 65 to help you.

infinitive		perfect tense	
se réveiller	*to wake up*	je me suis réveillé(e)	*I woke up*
se laver	*to get washed*	je me suis lavé(e)	*I got washed*
s'habiller	*to get dressed*	je me suis habillé(e)	*I got dressed*
se coucher	*to go to bed*	je me suis couché(e)	*I went to bed*

EXERCICE 15 Emilie tells you what her family did yesterday. Add the perfect tense of the verb given in brackets.

1 Nous … … … à sept heures. (se réveiller)

Example: Nous nous sommes réveillés à sept heures.

2 Madeleine … … … tout de suite. (se lever)

3 Elle … … … (se laver)

4 Elle … … … (s'habiller)

5 Moi, je … … … un peu plus tard. (se lever)

6 Je … … … (se laver)

7 Je … … … (s'habiller)

8 Mes parents … … … à six heures et demie. (se réveiller)

9 Ils … … … à dix heures du soir. (se coucher)

10 Nous … … … à neuf heures et demie. (se coucher)

4.7 The imperfect tense

You know that the <u>perfect tense</u> is the tense you use when talking about something that happened on one particular occasion in the past. If you want to talk about something that used to happen regularly or that went on for a length of time, then you use the <u>imperfect tense</u>.

You use the imperfect tense to:

* describe what something was like.
  When I <u>was</u> small, I <u>lived</u> in London.
  The houses <u>were</u> old.

* say what someone or something used to do.
  I <u>used to play</u> tennis.
  I <u>walked</u> to school.

* say what someone or something was doing when something else happened. This is often called an 'interrupted action'.
  John <u>was watching</u> television when the phone rang.

In English, the clues to the use of the imperfect tense are 'was/were' and 'used to'. If you would use those words to say something in English, you probably need the imperfect to say the same thing in French.

To form the imperfect tense,

* start with the 'nous' form of the present tense:
  nous jouons, nous dormons, nous finissons, nous répondons

* take off the **–ons**:
  jou–, dorm–, finiss–, répond–

* add these endings: **–ais , –ais, –ait, –ions, –iez, –aient**

* to give, for example:

jouer – *to play*	
je jou**ais**	nous jou**ions**
tu jou**ais**	vous jou**iez**
il/elle jou**ait**	ils/elles jou**aient**

je jouais	*I was playing/I used to play*
je dormais	*I was sleeping/I used to sleep*
je finissais	*I was finishing/I used to finish*
je répondais	*I was answering/I used to answer*

The good news about the imperfect tense is that you only have to learn one set of endings and these can be used with all verbs. So once you know how to find the stem (from the present tense 'nous' form) you can form the imperfect of any verb.

EXERCICE 1   What were they doing when the lights went out? Give the imperfect of the verbs in brackets and then translate the sentences into English.

1 Je … (jouer) aux cartes avec mon petit frère.
2 Nous … (parler)
3 Vous … (regarder) la télé.
4 Mes sœurs … (écouter) de la musique.
5 Tu … (dormir)
6 Mon père … (monter) l'escalier.
7 François … (entrer) dans la maison.
8 Maman … (préparer) le repas.
9 Jean … (travailler) dans le bureau.
10 Nicolas … (laver) la vaisselle.

The imperfect tense: irregular verbs

In the imperfect, even irregular verbs are easy to learn.

infinitive	present tense 'nous' form	imperfect tense 'je' form	translation
avoir	avons	j'avais	I had/used to have
aller	allons	j'allais	I was going/used to go
boire	buvons	je buvais	I was drinking/used to drink
manger	mangeons	je mangeais	I was eating/used to eat
lire	lisons	je lisais	I was reading/used to read
faire	faisons	je faisais	I was doing/used to do
être	sommes	j'étais	I was/used to be

EXERCICE 2 Change the verb in brackets into the imperfect tense.

1 Je … (manger) du gâteau.

2 Tu … (écouter) la radio.

3 Il … (faire) ses devoirs.

4 Elle … (porter) une robe.

5 Nous … (lire) des magazines.

6 Vous … (sortir) de la maison.

7 Ils … (boire) du café.

8 Nous … (être) contents.

9 Vous … (aller) en ville.

10 Ils … (avoir) une nouvelle voiture.

EXERCICE 3 Which tense should you use, the perfect or the imperfect? Look back to pages 59 and 67 to remind yourself when to use each one. Then read about Françoise's day out and for each underlined phrase, decide whether to use the perfect or the imperfect.

Samedi dernier, je suis allée/j'allais me promener en montagne. Nous sommes partis/partions à 7 heures du matin. Il a fait/faisait très beau et je n'ai pas pris/ne prenais pas ma veste. Mais soudain le temps a changé/changeait et il a plu/pleuvait tout l'après-midi. Ç'a été/C'était affreux. J'ai appris/J'apprenais ma leçon — à l'avenir je serai prête pour tous les temps.

EXERCICE 4 You need to use both the imperfect and the perfect in these sentences. Remember you use the imperfect for the action that was ongoing and the perfect for the action that 'interrupted' it.

1 Nous (dormir) quand le réveil (sonner).
   Example: Nous dormions quand le réveil a sonné.

2 Je (être) au cinéma quand il (arriver).

3 Il (avoir) un accident quand il (avoir) dix ans.

4 Les enfants (jouer) dans le parc quand il (commencer) à pleuvoir.

5 Tu (sortir) le chien quand il (venir).

4.8 Talking about the future

You use the future to talk about something that is going to happen, something you want to do or are going to do in the future.

In French there are two ways of talking about the future, just as in English: you can say something is 'going to happen', using *aller* and an infinitive – as explained below – or you can use verbs in the future tense, equivalent to the English 'will happen' – see page 70.

Aller + infinitive

This is the equivalent of the English 'to be going to ': 'I'm going to watch TV', 'He's going to play tennis', and so on. It is made up of the present tense of *aller* (to go) and the infinitive, just as it is in English:

Je vais jouer au tennis. *I'm going to play tennis.*

This way of expressing the future is the one most frequently used in conversation, especially when talking about the near future: this evening, tomorrow, the next few days. Read these examples:

Je vais faire mes devoirs.	*I'm going to do my homework.*
Tu vas regarder l'émission?	*Are you going to watch the programme?*
Il va jouer au tennis.	*He's going to play tennis.*
Nous allons prendre le petit déjeuner.	*We're going to have our breakfast.*
Vous allez faire du vélo?	*Are you going to go for a bike ride?*
Ils vont faire du ski.	*They're going to go skiing.*

EXERCICE 1 What are these people going to do? Complete the sentences by adding the correct part of *aller*.

1 Je ... faire mes devoirs.
2 Tu ... lire des magazines.
3 Il ... regarder la télé.
4 Nous ... jouer aux cartes.
5 Vous ... manger au resto.

6 Ils ... faire du ski.
7 Nous ... prendre le bus.
8 Je ... rester à la maison.
9 Tu ... réparer ton vélo.
10 Elle ... trouver ses affaires.

EXERCICE 2 What are your friends going to do for your birthday? Add the missing part of *aller* each time.

1 Yann ... faire un gâteau.
2 Yves et Thomas ... acheter des cadeaux.
3 Véronique ... décorer la salle.

4 Marceline ... mettre la table.
5 Benoît ... aider Marceline.
6 Ils ... tous chanter Bon anniversaire.

The future tense

This is the 'real' future tense. It translates the English 'will happen', 'will do' and can imply intention as well as future action. If you use the future 'will' in English, you need to use the future tense in French.

The future tense is quite easy to learn as most verbs are regular! It is made by adding these endings to the infinitive (for **-re** verbs take the **-e** off first): **-ai, -as, -a, -ons, -ez, -ont**.

	-er jouer	**-ir** finir	**-re** répondre → répondr-
je	jouerai	finirai	répondrai
tu	joueras	finiras	répondras
il/elle	jouera	finira	répondra
nous	jouerons	finirons	répondrons
vous	jouerez	finirez	répondrez
ils/elles	joueront	finiront	répondront

Remember that the endings are the same for all verb types, so once you've learnt them, as long as you know what the stem is (the infinitive minus any final **-e**), you'll be able to form the future tense easily.

EXERCICE 3 They've won the lottery! What will they choose? Complete by adding the right part of the verb *choisir*.

1 Mes parents … un nouvel appartement. *Example: choisiront*
2 Nous … une nouvelle voiture.
3 Jean-Paul … un VTT.
4 Je … une caméra.
5 Tu … des vêtements.
6 Françoise … une moto.
7 Nicolas … un bateau à voile.
8 Mes grands-parents … des plantes pour le jardin.
9 Je … des cadeaux pour mes copains.
10 Qu'est-ce que vous … ?

EXERCICE 4 L'anniversaire de maman. What will they do for mother's birthday? Put the verbs into the future tense.

1 Je lui … (offrir) une carte et des fleurs.
2 Mon père … (préparer) le repas.
3 Mon petit frère … (mettre) la table.
4 Nous … (manger) sur la terrasse.
5 Ma petite sœur … (débarrasser) la table.
6 Je … (laver) sa voiture.
7 Mon grand frère … (passer) l'aspirateur.
8 Nous … (inviter) son amie.
9 Les grands-parents … (arriver) vers midi.
10 A quelle heure … (arriver)-vous?

The future tense: irregular verbs

Some of the most common verbs are irregular in the future tense: they still use the endings shown above, but they use a different stem instead of their infinitive. The ones shown below are the ones you are likely to need most often, so it is best to try to learn them straight away. Learn the stem and work out how the regular endings shown on page 70 are used here too.

infinitive	stem	future tense
avoir	aur-	j'aurai, tu auras, il/elle aura, nous aurons, vous aurez, ils/elles auront
être	ser-	je serai, tu seras, etc.
aller	ir-	j'irai, tu iras, etc.
devoir	devr-	je devrai, tu devras
faire	fer-	je ferai, tu feras
pouvoir	pourr-	je pourrai, tu pourras
savoir	saur-	je saurai, tu sauras
venir	viendr-	je viendrai, tu viendras
voir	verr-	je verrai, tu verras
vouloir	voudr-	je voudrai, tu voudras

EXERCICE 5 Use the table above to help you put the verbs in brackets into the future tense:

1 j' (avoir)
2 vous (aller)
3 tu (venir)
4 nous (vouloir)

5 il (faire)
6 elle (voir)
7 ils (être)
8 nous (devoir)

9 vous (savoir)
10 elles (faire)

EXERCICE 6 Complete these sentences by adding the future tense of the verb in brackets:

1 Il … demain. (voir)
2 Nous … à Paris. (aller)
3 J' … de l'argent. (avoir)
4 Ils … du parapente. (faire)
5 Elle … après-demain. (venir)
6 Les élèves … sages! (être)

7 Vous … emporter quelque chose à manger. (vouloir)
8 Elles … besoin de quelque chose à boire. (avoir)
9 Tu … content! (être)
10 Je … faire mes devoirs. (devoir)

EXERCICE 7 What does the future have on offer for you? Complete the sentences and find out!

Votre horoscope pour la semaine prochaine

Capricorne
Tu … un voyage autour du monde. (faire)

Verseau
Tu … plus indépendant(e) et plus créatif/ve. (être)

Poisson
Tu … une solution à tes problèmes. (trouver)

Bélier
Tu … au cinéma avec un nouveau copain/une nouvelle copine. (aller)

Taureau
Tu … la réponse à une question qui te trouble. (savoir)

Gémeaux
Tu … la forme. (avoir)

Cancer
Tu n' … jamais la défaite. (accepter)

Lion
Tu … plus patient(e). (devenir)

Vierge
Tu … un ancien ami/une ancienne amie. (voir)

Balance
Tu … organiser tes affaires. (devoir)

Scorpion
Tu … de la chance. (avoir)

Sagittaire
Les planètes te … plus confiant(e). (rendre)

4.9 The conditional

The conditional is used to say what would or could happen. You generally need the conditional if you want to say phrases like 'I would ...' or 'I'd ...' or 'would you ...?' or 'could you ...?'.

It is formed by adding these endings to the infinitive (for **-re** verbs take the **-e** off first): **-ais, -ais, -ait, -ions, -iez, -aient**.

	-er jouer	**-ir** finir	**-re** répondre → répondr-
je	jouerais	finirais	répondrais
tu	jouerais	finirais	répondrais
il/elle	jouerait	finirait	répondrait
nous	jouerions	finirions	répondrions
vous	joueriez	finiriez	répondriez
ils/elles	joueraient	finiraient	répondraient

Look back to page 70 to compare this pattern with the <u>future tense</u>. Compare the stem and compare the endings. What do you notice?

Now look back to page 67 and compare the conditional stem and endings with the stem and endings of the <u>imperfect tense</u>. Again, what do you notice?

The conditional is used where there is some doubt about an action, or some other condition is involved:

J'aimerais sortir demain. *I'd like to go out tomorrow.*

Je finirais vite si tu m'aidais. *I would finish quickly if you helped me.*

It is also used to make polite requests:

Pourriez-vous ouvrir la fenêtre? *Could you open the window?*

Je voudrais un kilo de pommes. *I'd like a kilo of apples.*

The conditional: irregular verbs

These common irregular verbs work in the same way as in the future tense: the same stem is used, but with the conditional endings. You are very likely to come across these verbs in the conditional, so be ready to recognise them and to use the most common forms.

infinitive	stem	conditional	translation
avoir	aur-	j'aurais	*I would have*
être	ser-	je serais	*I would be*
aller	ir-	j'irais	*I would go*
devoir	devr-	je devrais	*I would have to/I should*
faire	fer-	je ferais	*I would do*
pouvoir	pourr-	je pourrais	*I would be able to/I could*
savoir	saur-	je saurais	*I would know*
venir	viendr-	je viendrais	*I would come*
voir	verr-	je verrais	*I would see*
vouloir	voudr-	je voudrais	*I would like*

> **Il y aurait** trop de monde. *There would be too many people.*
>
> **Ce serait** très bien. *That would be very good.*
>
> **Pourriez-vous** m'aider? *Could you help me?*

EXERCICE 1 Complete these sentences using the conditional of the verb in brackets.

1 (vouloir) Je … une baguette.

2 (aller) J' … en ville s'il faisait beau.

3 (faire) Je … mes devoirs si j'avais mes cahiers.

4 (être) Je … content de vous voir.

5 (pouvoir) Je … voter si j'avais dix-huit ans.

6 (devoir) J'ai mal aux dents, je … aller chez le dentiste.

4.10 Negatives

Negatives and the present tense

The negative is used when you want to say 'no' or 'not'. In the present tense in English, we often use 'don't', 'can't', 'haven't', and so on, to make a negative statement: 'I don't know.' 'He can't swim.' 'They haven't any children.'

To form the negative in French, you put *ne* in front of the verb and *pas* after it:

| ne | + | verb | + | pas |

Je ne sais pas.

Il ne nage pas.

Ils n'ont pas d'enfants.

Ne … pas also affects what comes afterwards. In French *un / une / du / de la / de l' / des* all change to *de* or *d'* in a negative sentence.

Il a un chien.   Il n'a pas de chien.

EXERCICE 1 Now make these phrases negative by putting *ne* in front of and *pas* after the verb. Don't forget to look out for *un / une / du / de la / des* and change them to *de*.

1 Elle fait du vélo.

2 Nous avons un animal à la maison.

3 J'ai une sœur.

4 Il a un frère.

5 Ils vont au collège.

6 Nous faisons du parapente.

7 Vous mangez des fraises?

8 Ils ont des enfants.

9 Tu as un chat?

10 Il va au lit.

Negatives and the perfect tense

To form the negative in the perfect tense, you use exactly the same construction as in the present tense: *ne … pas*. *Ne* goes in front of the auxiliary (*avoir* or *être*) and *pas* directly after it. The past participle (*regardé*, *fait*, *venu*, etc.) follows *pas*.

Je **n'ai pas fait** mes devoirs.

ne	+	avoir/être	+	pas	+	past participle

Il **n'est pas allé** au cinéma.

Nous **n'avons pas joué** au foot.

EXERCICE 2 Make these statements negative. Don't forget that after *ne … pas, un / une / du / de la / des* all become *de* or *d'*.

1 Stéphanie est allée au cinéma.
   Example: Stéphanie n'est pas allée au cinéma.
2 Nous sommes allés au restaurant.
3 Marc a commandé une pizza.
4 Sandrine a mangé des frites.
5 Les garçons ont bu du vin.
6 J'ai fumé une cigarette.
7 Mes parents sont sortis.
8 Vous avez vu le film 'Titanic'?
9 Tu as reçu une lettre.
10 Nous avons raté le bus.

Useful negative expressions

There are other negative expressions which also use *ne* in front of the verb and another word after it. Here are two very useful ones.

ne … jamais *never* Je ne mange jamais de sucre. *I never eat sugar.*

EXERCICE 3 Imagine someone is asking you these questions. Answer them using *ne … jamais*. Don't forget to change the verb form from *tu* to *je*.

1 Tu joues au foot?
   Example: Non, je ne joue jamais au foot.
2 Tu manges des escargots?
3 Tu regardes la télé?
4 Tu fumes des cigarettes?
5 Tu bois du vin?
6 Tu ranges ta chambre?

ne … plus *no longer/no more* Je ne joue plus du piano. *I don't play the piano any more.*

EXERCICE 4 How would you say that these people no longer do these things? Put *ne … plus* around the verb.

1 Mon père joue au football.
   Example: Mon père ne joue plus au football.
2 Ma mère fait de la planche à voile.
3 Mes sœurs mangent de la viande.
4 Tu fumes des cigarettes?
5 Nous buvons du vin.
6 J'ai de l'argent.

5 Adverbs

An adverb is a word which describes a verb. It adds meaning to the verb and describes how an action is done.

He drove <u>quickly</u>.

They walk <u>slowly</u>.

He speaks <u>clearly</u>.

He speaks French <u>well</u>.

To work out if a word is an adverb, ask yourself the question, 'Does it describe the action?' So, how did he drive? – using an adverb, 'quickly'.

Some adverbs add information about where, when and to what extent: 'far', 'soon' and 'very' are all adverbs. Look out for the letters *adv* in a dictionary to help you identify these words.

In English, adverbs are usually made by adding **-ly** to an adjective:

slow + -ly = slowly

☞ 3.1 Most French adverbs are made by adding **-ment** to the feminine form of an adjective. (See pages 23–29 for feminine adjective endings.)

lent + -e = -ment = lentement

Ils marchent lentement. *They walk slowly*.

The adjectives in this table all have regular feminine forms. Look at how each one forms an adverb.

adjective			adverb	
masculine	feminine			
clair	claire	*clear*	clairement	*clearly*
final	finale	*final*	finalement	*finally*
triste	triste	*sad*	tristement	*sadly*

It works in the same way for irregular adjectives, as you can see in the next table. Once you know the feminine form of the adjective, you just add **-ment**.

adjective			adverb	
masculine	feminine			
doux	douce	*soft/sweet*	doucement	*softly/sweetly*
fier	fière	*proud*	fièrement	*proudly*
franc	franche	*frank*	franchement	*frankly*
heureux	heureuse	*happy*	heureusement	*luckily*

EXERCICE 1 How would you form the adverbs from these adjectives? Here's a hint: 1–6 have regular feminine forms, 7–12 are irregular. (If you can't remember the rules for feminine adjective endings, look back to pages 23–29.)

1 triste … (*sadly*)

2 facile … (*easily*)

3 difficile … (*with difficulty*)

4 parfait … (*perfectly*)

5 direct … (*directly*)

6 normal … (*normally*)

7 doux … (*softly/sweetly*)

8 sérieux … (*seriously*)

9 heureux … (*luckily*)

10 actif … (*actively*)

11 traditionnel … (*traditionally*)

12 nouveau … (*recently*)

EXERCICE 2 Now complete the following phrases. Use the underlined adjective to make an adverb to fill the gap. Check whether the adjective is already in the feminine singular, and if not, change it before adding **-ment**.

1 Sa vie est <u>dangereuse</u>. Il vit …

2 Elle est <u>fière</u> de lui. Elle parle de lui …

3 Il trouve cet exercice <u>facile</u>. Il le fait …

4 Il est <u>probable</u> qu'il va pleuvoir. Est-ce qu'il va pleuvoir? Oui, …

5 Elle a une voix <u>douce</u>. Elle chante …

6 Les professeurs sont <u>francs</u> avec nous. Ils parlent …

Exceptions

There are of course exceptions to the **-e** + **-ment** rule.

Adjectives which end in **i** or **u** form their adverb from the masculine form:

adjective masculine		adverb	
vrai	*true/real*	vraiment	*truly/really*
poli	*polite*	poliment	*politely*
joli	*pretty*	joliment	*attractively*
absolu	*absolute*	absolument	*absolutely*
gentil*	*kind*	gentiment	*nicely*

* Note that *gentil* loses its final **l** too.

EXERCICE 3 Choose a suitable adverb from the box on page 76 to complete each sentence.

1 C'est vrai qu'il ne pleut pas! Il ne
   pleut … pas.

2 Il est très poli. Il répond …

3 Elle a une jolie voix. Elle parle …

4 Cet enfant est gentil. Il joue …
   avec le bébé.

A few adjectives need an accent on the **-e** when they become adverbs. This makes them easier to pronounce.

adjective		adverb	
masculine	feminine		
énorme	énorme	énormément	enormously
profond	profonde	profondément	deeply
précis	précise	précisément	precisely

EXERCICE 4 Choose an adverb from the list above to complete each sentence.

1 Il est très précis quand il parle.
   Il parle ….

2 Sa fortune est énorme. Ça me
   plaît …….

3 Quand il dort on ne peut pas le
   réveiller. Il dort ….

5.1 Common irregular adverbs

There are a few adverbs that look very different from their corresponding adjectives. The ones listed are used frequently so you'll probably recognise them, but you need to learn them.

adjective		adverb	
bon	good	bien	well
mauvais	bad	mal	badly
rapide	quick	vite	quickly
petit	small	peu	little
meilleur*	better	mieux*	better

☞ 3.9 * For more on *meilleur* and *mieux*, see page 41.

EXERCICE 1 One sentence in each pair contains an adjective and the other an adverb. Can you identify them? Remember: an adjective describes a noun and an adverb describes a verb.

1a Ce repas est bon. *This meal is good.*

1b Il mange bien. *He eats well. Example: 1a adjective = bon, 1b adverb = bien*

2a Le poisson est mauvais. *The fish is bad.*

2b Les enfants mangent mal. *The children eat badly.*

3a Il travaille mieux que moi. *He works better than I do.*

3b Cette émission est meilleure que l'autre. *This programme is better than the other.*

4a C'est un train rapide. *It's a fast train.*

4b Il va vite. *It goes quickly.*

5a Michel a trouvé un petit boulot. *Michel has found a small job.*

5b Pour commencer, il travaille peu mais il regarde. *To begin with, he doesn't work much (works little) but he watches.*

EXERCICE 2 Now find the adjective in the first sentence each time. Make it into an adverb to fill the gap in the second sentence.

1 Daniel est meilleur chanteur que moi. Il chante … que moi.

2 Il a fait un mauvais travail. Il travaille …

3 Votre français est très bon. Vous parlez … le français.

4 Mme Goddard a une voiture rapide. Elle va …

EXERCICE 3 Look back at all the patterns for forming adverbs that you have learnt. Then fill in the adjectives and matching adverbs in these sentences.

1 Mon frère est mécanicien. Il a un … travail. Il travaille … (*good/well*)

2 La vieille dame est … Elle regarde les enfants … (*sad/sadly*)

3 Le repas est … Tu cuisines … (*perfect/perfectly*)

4 Antoine est toujours … Même quand il joue, il joue … (*serious/seriously*)

5 Il fait …, il pleut, et l'équipe joue … (*bad/badly*)

There are other adverbs that do not have corresponding adjectives. Again, they are common words which you will probably recognise. They give information about time, place, quantity. Here are some of the most useful ones:

bientôt *soon*	demain *tomorrow*	assez *enough/quite*
souvent *often*	loin *far*	beaucoup *a lot*
soudain *suddenly*	près *near*	très *very*

EXERCICE 4 Read this account of a family wedding and use the adverbs in the box to fill the gaps.

bien	bientôt	finalement	heureusement
mieux	soudain	très	

Samedi, je suis allée au mariage de ma cousine. Tout allait bien et …, mon oncle a eu … mal au ventre. Il ne se sentait pas … du tout. …, le marié était médecin! Il lui a donné quelque chose et … il s'est senti …

… le mariage a continué comme si rien ne s'était passé.

6 Prepositions

Prepositions are short words which come in front of a noun or pronoun to provide important information in a sentence. For example:

'We met in the café at 6 p.m.' – this sentence has two prepositions, 'in' and 'at'.

Prepositions are used to say:

- where a person or thing is: **sur** la table (on the table), **à** l'école (at school)
- when something happens: **à** midi (at midday), **dans** une minute (in a minute), **après** le week-end (after the weekend)
- how something happens: **avec** hésitation (hesitantly), **sans** lui (without him)
- who something is for: **pour** moi (for me)
- who something belongs to: le vélo **de** Paul (Paul's bike) … and other similar interesting details.

The most useful prepositions in French are presented below. The two that are used most frequently à and de.

6.1 À

À is used sometimes on its own and sometimes combined with the definite article (*le, la, l', les*). You need to learn which to use when.

With the definite article, the masculine form is *au* and the plural is *aux*.

à + le	=	**au**	Je vais au collège.
à + la	=	**à la**	Je vais à la banque.
à + l'	=	**à l'**	Je vais à l'église/à l'institut.
à + les	=	**aux**	Je vais aux toilettes.

À has various meanings and can be used to express place, manner, time, possession.

- place

  Je suis à la maison. *I'm at home.*

  Je vais au collège. *I'm going to school.*

  Pour aller à la plage? *How do you get to the beach?*

  Il habite à la campagne. *He lives in the country.*

  Je vais au Canada. *I'm going to Canada.*

  aux Etats–Unis *in/to the United States*

  Elle habite à Nice. *She lives in Nice.*

Note that you use *à* with town names but *au/à la/à l'/aux* with masculine countries. (Feminine countries use en instead: *en Allemagne.*)

● manner, description

un sandwich au fromage *a cheese sandwich*

une glace à la vanille *vanilla ice cream*

un garçon aux cheveux blonds *a boy with fair hair*

● time

Les cours commencent à neuf heures. *Lessons begin at 9 a.m.*

☞ 2.3 ● possession (see page 21 in Pronouns for more on this)

C'est à qui? *Whose is it?*

C'est à moi! *It's mine!*

C'est à Christophe. *It's Christophe's.*

EXERCICE 1 Write out five sentences saying where you are going, using *au, à la* or *à l'*.
Start with: *Je vais …*

1 la plage   **3** la piscine   **5** l'auberge de jeunesse

2 le collège   **4** le jardin public

EXERCICE 2 Now write out how you would ask the way to these places: *Pour aller à … ?*

1 l'église St-Ouen   **4** l'hôtel de ville

2 la cathédrale Jeanne-d'Arc   **5** les toilettes

3 le Gros Horloge

EXERCICE 3 Towns, cities, countries … Copy and complete the sentences, deciding whether
they need just *à* or *au/à l'/aux*.

1 Notre-Dame est … Paris.

2 Buckingham Palace est … Londres.

3 Mes amis habitent … Canada.

4 Tokyo se trouve … Japon.

5 Il y a un grand port … Marseille.

6 Le mont Blanc est … Chamonix.

7 Les bureaux de la CE se trouvent … Luxembourg.

8 Il fait chaud … Etats-Unis.

9 Mon ami habite … New York.

10 On parle français … Québec.

EXERCICE 4 Complete this description of the Peugeot family, filling the gaps with *à* or *à* plus
le, la, l', les.

La famille Peugeot habite … Paris. Leur fille Aurélie fait ses études … Etats-Unis.
Leur fils Nicolas travaille … Canada. Mme Peugeot travaille … musée du Louvre.
M. Peugeot travaille … aéroport de Roissy. Pour les grandes vacances, ils vont …
Nice.

EXERCICE 5 What sort of ice cream would you like? Write out six sentences choosing a flavour. *Example: Je voudrais une glace au citron.*

la fraise   la banane   l'orange

le citron   les raisins secs   le chocolat

EXERCICE 6 And what sort of sandwich would you like? Complete the sentence five times to choose these different fillings. Start off with: *Je voudrais un sandwich …*

1 jambon   4 tomates

2 poulet   5 fromage

3 saucisson

EXERCICE 7 Now try adding *à* to the following sentences. Some of them need the definite article and some don't.

1 Les enfants vont … plage.

2 Quelqu'un a frappé … porte.

3 Le film commence … 19 h 45.

4 Avez–vous un sandwich … fromage?

5 J'adore la tarte … pommes.

6 Ils passent les vacances … Etats–Unis.

7 Le train arrive … 11 h 25.

8 Il boit un café … lait.

9 Ils se retrouvent … arrêt d'autobus.

10 La trousse bleue est … moi.

6.2 *De*

De is often used on its own and sometimes combined with the definite article (*le*, *la*, *l'*, *les*). When combined with *le* or *les*, it changes to *du* or *des*.

de + le = du

de + la = de la

de + l' = de l'

de + les = des

De can be used to mean:

● of

C'est la voiture de mon père. *It's my father's car. (literally, the car of my father)*
Voici ton cadeau d'anniversaire. *Here's your birthday present.*

☞ 1.4 ● **of** – in expressions of quantity

Je voudrais du beurre et de la confiture. *I'd like some butter and some jam.*

(Look back to page 13 on the 'partitive article', to see how this works.)

Il y a des cerises. *There are some cherries.*

(Look back to page 11, 'How to say some'.)

● **from**

Il vient d'Edimbourg. *He comes from Edinburgh.*

Je rentre de l'école à 16 heures. *I come home from school at 4 p.m.*

du 8 au 12 avril *from the 8th to the 12th of April*

● **with**

La plage est couverte de sable. *The beach is covered with sand.*

EXERCICE 1 Add *de* to these sentences and translate them.

1 C'est la bicyclette … ma sœur.

2 Ils viennent … Londres.

3 Les montagnes sont couvertes …
neige.

4 C'est le mois … décembre.

5 Ce sont les vacances … Noël.

EXERCICE 2 Put *du/de la/de l'/des* in the following sentences about some visitors to Paris, and then translate them.

1 Les touristes viennent … Japon.

2 Ils prennent des photos … tour
Eiffel.

3 Il y a une belle vue … ville de Paris.

4 Ils visitent le musée … Louvre.

5 Ils font un tour … monuments.

Prepositional phrases using *de*

These tell you where something or someone is. They are called phrases because they are made up of more than one word, so for example 'in front of' is a prepositional phrase in English because it is made up of three words.

en face de	*opposite*
près de	*near*
loin de	*far from*
à côté de	*beside/next to*
au-dessus de	*above*
au-dessous de	*below/beneath*

EXERCICE 3 How would you tell someone where the nearest phone box is? Start with: *Il y a une cabine téléphonique …*

1 near the station (*la gare*)

2 far from here (*ici*)

3 opposite the church (*l'église*)

4 beside the bus stop (*l'arrêt de bus*)

EXERCICE 4   *Où est le restaurant?* There are six restaurants in this town. Can you say where each one is? *Example: Il y a un restaurant au-dessus de la boutique.*

Expressions of quantity using *de*

In these expressions *de* is always used on its own and not combined with the definite article.

un kilo de	*a kilo of*
une bouteille de	*a bottle of*
une boîte de	*a tin/can of*
un litre de	*a litre of*

assez de	*enough (of)*	Il a assez d'argent. *He has enough money.*
beaucoup de	*a lot of*	J'ai beaucoup de copains. *I have a lot of friends.*
moins de	*less*	Elle a moins d'argent que lui. *She has less money than him.*
plus de	*more*	La tour Eiffel a plus de cent ans. *The Eiffel tower is more than 100 years old.*
trop de	*too much/ too many*	Elle fait trop de fautes. *She makes too many mistakes.*

EXERCICE 5   How would you ask for these?

Example: Je voudrais une bouteille de vin rouge.

EXERCICE 6   How would you say that …?

… you have lots of these:

1 livres
2 BD
3 cassettes
4 chaussettes
5 copains

… you have enough of these:

6 crayons
7 frites
8 bonbons
9 pulls
10 baskets

… you have too much/ too many of these:

11 devoirs
12 travail
13 limonade
14 frites
15 sucre

6.3 Other prepositions

Saying where something is

chez *at the house / shop / business of*

chez moi *at my house*
chez lui/elle *at his / her house*
chez eux *at their house*

dans *in*

dans la maison *in the house*

derrière *behind*

derrière la porte *behind the door*

devant *in front of*

devant le cinéma *in front of the cinema*

en *in*

Il est en ville. *He is in town.*
Elle habite en Espagne. *She lives in Spain.*

Note: use *en* for feminine countries: *en France, en Grande-Bretagne*
but use *au/aux* for masculine countries: *au Portugal*

entre *between*

entre le cinéma et le café *between the cinema and the café*

sous *under*

sous le pont *under the bridge*

sur *on*

sur la table *on the table*

EXERCICE 1 Où est Jean-Luc? Find the right picture for each statement.

1 Il est sous la douche.

2 Il est derrière la porte.

3 Il est devant la maison.

4 Il est entre la poste et la banque.

5 Il est sur le pont.

6 Il est dans la cuisine.

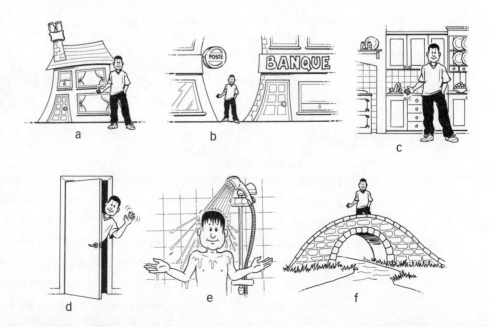

a   b   c

d   e   f

EXERCICE 2 Choose a preposition from the list on page 84 to add to each caption to say where the dog is.

Le chien est … la table.

Le chien est … le lit.

Le chien est … le placard.

Le chien est … la cheminée.

Le chien est … la porte.

Saying when something happens

à *at*

à dix heures *at ten o'clock*

après *after*

après le petit déjeuner *after breakfast*
après avoir fait la vaisselle *after doing the washing up*

avant *before*

avant la récréation *before breaktime*
avant d'aller au collège *before going to school*

depuis *for/since*

depuis deux ans *for two years*
depuis les vacances *since the holidays*

en *in*

Son anniversaire est en juillet.
His birthday is in July.

pendant *during*

pendant la journée *during the day*

pour *for*

pour une semaine *for a week*

vers *about*

vers dix heures *about ten o'clock*

Il habite ici depuis trois ans.
He has been living here for three years.

EXERCICE 3 Answer the questions using the information in brackets. Use a full sentence and the appropriate preposition.

1 Simon se lève à quelle heure? (7.30) *Example: Il se lève à 7 heures 30.*

2 Quand prend-il sa douche? (before breakfast)

3 Quand va-t-il au collège? (after breakfast)

4 A quelle heure rentre-t-il? (16.30)

5 Quand dîne-t-il? (about 7 p.m.)

6 Quand fait-il ses devoirs? (before going to bed)

7 Quand dort-il? (during the night)

8 Il va à Paris pour combien de temps? (1 week)

7 Revision

These exercises revise and practise the grammar you have learnt in this book. Look back at the relevant chapter as often as you need to, to help you do the exercises.

★ Sentences marked with a star summarise some key grammar points. You can check for yourself that you've learnt those key points by completing the sentences.

1 Nouns

★ Can you fill the gaps in this sentence?
In French all nouns are ... or ... , as shown in a dictionary by (*m*) or (*f*).

EXERCICE 1 These nouns are all words for people: decide whether they are masculine or feminine and copy them out adding *m* or *f* after each one.

1 frère	**3** mère	**5** fille
2 sœur	**4** père	**6** garçon

★ The word for 'a' in front of masculine nouns is ...
and in front of feminine nouns is ...

EXERCICE 2 What have you got in your bag? Add all these things to the sentence, with the correct word for 'a' in front of each one.
Dans mon sac, j'ai une trousse, ...

1 trousse (*f*)	**3** dictionnaire (*m*)	**5** tee-shirt (*m*)
2 stylo (*m*)	**4** serviette (*f*)	**6** pomme (*f*)

★ The word for 'the' in front of masculine nouns is ...
and in front of feminine nouns is ...
You use *l'* in front of nouns which begin with ...
To say 'the' with plural nouns, both masculine and feminine, you use ...

EXERCICE 3   Are these nouns masculine or feminine, singular or plural? If you can't remember, use a dictionary. Copy out the words, putting *le*, *la*, *l'* or *les* in front of them.

1 ville
2 maison
3 collège
4 école
5 rues

6 hôpital
7 plage
8 magasins
9 château
10 gare

EXERCICE 4   Can you remember how to make the plural of these words? Look back at the rules on pages 10–12 to help you.

1 le château
2 l'oiseau
3 le journal
4 l'animal
5 le nez

6 le genou
7 le gâteau
8 le bateau
9 le fils
10 le cheval

★   The partitive article refers to a part of something, an unspecified quantity. In English we say 'some' or 'any', in French we use …, … or …

EXERCICE 5   Copy out these questions, filling the gaps with *du*, *de la* or *de l'*.

1 Avez vous … pain?
2 Est-ce qu'il y a … confiture?
3 Tu prends … sucre?

4 Qui veut … eau?
5 Qui veut … salade?

2   Pronouns

EXERCICE 1   Copy out the text inserting the correct **subject pronoun** in each gap.

… m'appelle Céline. … ai un frère. … a douze ans et … est très sportif. J'ai aussi une sœur. … a cinq ans. … est très petite.

Mes parents sont belges mais … travaillent en France. … habitons à Paris.

Ma mère et ma sœur se ressemblent beaucoup. … ont les cheveux roux.

As-… des frères ou des sœurs? … êtes combien dans la famille? Où habitez-…?

EXERCICE 2   Can you find the **direct object pronouns** in these sentences?

1 Il le cherche.
2 Je les regarde.
3 Ludovic l'a perdu.
4 Il m'a vu.
5 Elle t'a trouvé.
6 Il nous voit.

7 Je vous invite à dîner chez moi samedi.
8 Je ne l'aime pas.
9 Nicolas ne les mange pas.
10 Il les déteste.

EXERCICE 3 Which **direct object pronoun** do you need? Translate the sentences, remembering to put the pronoun (underlined) in front of the verb. You'll need the verbs *voir*, *chercher* and *aimer*.

1 He sees <u>me</u>. *Example: Il me voit.*
2 I see <u>him</u>.
3 They see <u>us</u>.
4 I am looking for <u>you</u>.
5 They are looking for <u>us</u>.

6 I don't like <u>them</u>.
7 They don't like <u>me</u>.
8 We like <u>them</u>.
9 Are you looking for <u>her</u>?
10 She's looking for <u>him</u>.

EXERCICE 4 Which are the **indirect object pronouns** in these sentences? Make a list of them and then translate the sentences.

1 Il me donne son livre.
2 Il me le donne.
3 Je lui passe mon stylo.
4 Je le lui passe.
5 Il te donne son dictionnaire.

6 Il te le donne.
7 Il nous offre un cadeau.
8 Il nous l'offre.
9 Je te prête mon vélo.
10 Je te le prête.

EXERCICE 5 Replace the underlined words with an **indirect object pronoun**. Then copy out the sentence, putting the pronoun in the correct place.

1 Je donne mon livre <u>à Jacques</u>.
 Example: lui, Je lui donne mon livre.
2 Il prête son stylo <u>à moi</u>.
3 Je donne mes tennis <u>à toi</u>.
4 Jacques donne l'argent <u>au garçon</u>.

5 Qu'est-ce qu'il donne <u>à toi</u>?
6 Il donne des bonbons <u>à nous</u>.
7 Nous donnons du chocolat <u>à vous</u>.
8 Le prof donne de bonnes notes <u>aux élèves</u>.

EXERCICE 6 Replace the underlined words with the correct **emphatic pronoun**.

1 Véronique vient en ville avec <u>ses parents</u>. *Example: Véronique vient en ville avec eux.*
2 Elle préfère aller au cinéma avec <u>mon amie et moi</u>.

3 J'ai acheté un cadeau pour <u>mon copain</u>.
4 Elle est sortie avec <u>ses copines</u>.
5 Qui va en ville avec <u>ton frère et toi</u>?
6 J'aimerais venir chez vous sans <u>ma sœur</u>.

3 Adjectives

★ Can you complete these sentences?
An adjective has to agree with …
This means it may have a different … when used with a masculine or feminine noun.

EXERCICE 1 Choose the correct adjective from the box to complete the sentences. (Remember to look at the adjective endings.)

grande   intelligente   petit   bruyants   bavardes

1 C'est une … ville.

2 Mes frères sont …

3 Mes sœurs sont …

4 Ma copine est …

5 L'appartement est …

EXERCICE 2 Complete the sentences by putting the adjectives in the correct form, adding **–e** and **–s** if necessary.

1 Les enfants sont (jeune).

2 Mon amie est (bavard).

3 Son frère est (marrant).

4 Elle est (triste).

5 Elle a deux (petit) sœurs.

6 Sa mère est (fatigué).

7 La ville est (moderne).

8 Les rues sont (sale).

9 Notre maison est (tranquille).

10 Les appartements sont (petit).

EXERCICE 3 Complete these sentences with the correct form of the adjective in brackets.

1 Le jambon est très (bon).

2 Les pigeons sont (gros).

3 J'habite une (vieux) maison.

4 Dans ma classe, il y a un (nouveau) élève.

5 Paul et Sylvie sont (paresseux).

6 J'habite une ville (ancien).

7 Les rues sont (étroit).

8 Les enfants sont (bruyant).

9 La vie ici est (traditionnel).

10 Mes mains sont (sec) en hiver.

11 L'année (dernier), je suis allé en Angleterre.

12 Ma grand-mère est (fier) de sa (beau) maison.

EXERCICE 4 **Possessive adjectives**

First, imagine you are describing your own family. Write out who the people and pets in the picture are, using *mon*, *ma* or *mes* for each one.

Example: Voici mon père. Voici mes chiens.

Now imagine you are describing your family on behalf of both you and your brother. Write out the list again using *notre* or *nos*.

★ If you want to say 'his father' or 'her father', you say … *père*.
If you want to say 'his mother' or 'her mother', you say … *mère*.
If you want to say 'his parents' or 'her parents', you say … *parents*.

EXERCICE 5 These objects belong to a friend of yours, Marcel. Write a short phrase about each one, using *son*, *sa* or *ses*.

Example: C'est son vélo, Ce sont ses affaires.

affaires   vélo   sac   vêtements   chaussures   photo   chat

EXERCICE 6 **Interrogative adjectives** Complete the following questions using *quel*, *quelle*, *quels* or *quelles*.

1 … billets voulez-vous?
2 Vous achetez … voiture?
3 Je prends … ligne?
4 C'est … arrêt de bus?

5 Tu pars … jour?
6 A … heure?
7 Tu prends … train?
8 Tu pars de … gare?

EXERCICE 7 Look at the illustration and read the bubbles. Someone's got a good idea, someone else has a better idea, so how would you say 'And I've got <u>the best</u> idea'?

J'ai une bonne idée

J'ai une meilleure idée

4   Verbs

★ Verbs are sometimes called … words.
In French, verb infinitives generally end in …, … and …
When you take off the last two letters, you are left with the …, which you use to form different tenses of the verb.

EXERCICE 1 Give the English meaning of these verbs and write out the stem of each one.

1 jouer *Example: to play, jou-*
2 parler
3 attendre
4 finir
5 vendre

6 ouvrir
7 fermer
8 dormir
9 habiter
10 aimer

EXERCICE 2 The present tense: **-er verbs** Put these infinitives into the present tense:

1 je (écouter) *Example: j'écoute*
2 il (parler)
3 nous (habiter)
4 tu (porter)
5 vous (regarder)
6 ils (manger)
7 tu (parler)
8 elles (aimer)

EXERCICE 3 The present tense: **-ir verbs** Give the correct part of these verbs:

1 il (choisir)
2 vous (sortir)
3 nous (finir)
4 je (partir)
5 ils (finir)
6 elles (réussir)
7 tu (dormir)
8 je (dormir)
9 nous (sentir)
10 Marc (remplir)

EXERCICE 4 The present tense: **-re verbs** Give the correct part of these verbs:

1 je (vendre)
2 nous (descendre)
3 ils (répondre)
4 vous (attendre)
5 tu (descendre)
6 Maxim (vendre)
7 Nathalie et Louise (répondre)
8 Gilbert (attendre)
9 les filles (descendre)
10 les garçons (attendre)

EXERCICE 5 The present tense: **irregular verbs** Complete the sentences with the correct part of *avoir* or *être*.

1 J'… douze ans.
2 Quel âge …-tu?
3 Nous … un chien.
4 Elle … fatiguée.
5 Ils … français.
6 Mon frère … quinze ans.
7 Je … britannique.
8 Vous … en retard.
9 Tous mes copains … treize ans.
10 Mon frère … sportif.

EXERCICE 6 Which verb would you use, *aller* or *faire*? Complete the sentences with the right part of the appropriate verb.

1 Je … mes devoirs.
2 Nous … en ville.
3 Il … de la planche à voile.
4 Je ne … pas au cinéma.
5 Où …- vous?
6 Que …-vous?
7 Tu … tes devoirs?
8 Mes parents … au travail.

★ Can you complete the sentences?
There is a category of verbs called reflexive verbs. They always have a …
between the subject and the verb. For example, in *Je me lève à 7 heures du matin*,
it is the word …

EXERCICE 7 **The present tense: reflexive verbs** Insert the correct reflexive pronoun to complete the sentences.

1 Je … lave tout de suite.

2 Ils … lavent.

3 Vous … réveillez à 8 heures.

4 Marceline … douche le soir.

5 Comment tu … appelles?

6 Elle … appelle Corinne.

EXERCICE 8 Fill the gap in each sentence with the right part of the verb in brackets.

1 Sylvie … les mains avant de faire la cuisine. (se laver)

2 Normalement, Jean-Luc et Paul … tôt. (se réveiller)

3 Je … dans ma chambre. (s'habiller)

4 Mes parents … à six heures. (se lever)

5 Vous … à quelle heure? (se coucher)

★ You use the perfect tense to talk about …

To form the perfect tense, you need two things: … and …

EXERCICE 9 **The perfect tense** Fill in the right part of the auxiliary verb *avoir*.

1 J'… mangé une banane.

2 Nous … regardé la télé.

3 Les enfants … parlé toute la journée.

4 Il … vendu sa maison.

5 Vous … choisi la robe jaune.

6 Ma copine … écouté toute l'émission.

7 Fabien … joué au tennis.

8 Tu … bien dormi?

EXERCICE 10 Complete each sentence with the perfect tense of the verb in brackets.

1 J' … … avec ma mère. (parler)

2 Nous … … les billets de train. (acheter)

3 Tu … … la radio hier soir? (écouter)

4 Ils … … leur voiture. (vendre)

5 Vous … … votre chien? (perdre)

6 Mon copain … … ses devoirs. (finir)

7 Les enfants … … sous la tente. (dormir)

8 Jean … … les bagages. (porter)

9 Ma mère … … une tarte aux fraises. (choisir)

10 Les garçons … … les chocolats. (manger)

EXERCICE 11 Complete each sentence with the perfect tense of the verb in brackets. Take care – they have irregular past participles.

1 J' … … un coca. (boire)

2 Il … … son magazine. (lire)

3 Vous … … beaucoup de cadeaux. (recevoir)

4 Ils … … un très bon film. (voir)

5 Joseph … … son cahier. (prendre)

6 Nous … … le CD. (mettre)

7 Elle … … son vocabulaire français. (apprendre)

8 J' … … à mon correspondant. (écrire)

9 Mon père me l' … … (dire)

10 Il n' … pas … le test. (comprendre)

★ Can you complete these sentences?

To form the perfect tense, most verbs put together the present tense of *avoir* and the … of the verb.

However, some verbs use the present tense of … instead of *avoir*.

Reflexive verbs use the present tense of …

★ See if you can write from memory a list of the 12 main verbs which take *être* in the perfect tense. (To help you, study the list on page 63 for one minute before you start!)

EXERCICE 12 Complete the sentences with the correct part of *être*.

1 Je … allé à l'école.

2 Nous … venus pour le repas.

3 Ils … arrivés tard.

4 Elle … allée toute seule.

5 Vous … partis en avance.

EXERCICE 13 Put the verb in brackets into the perfect tense, i.e. the correct part of *être* and the past participle. Don't forget that the past participle may need the feminine ending **–e** and the plural ending **–s**.

1 Je … … à dix heures. (sortir)

2 Nous … … le trois avril. (arriver)

3 Elle … … une semaine. (rester)

4 Ils … … tout de suite. (monter)

5 Je … … à quatre heures. (partir)

6 Les enfants … … malades. (tomber)

7 Mon grand-père … … l'an dernier. (mourir)

8 Elle … … le 25 juin. (naître)

9 Nous … … sans la clé. (entrer)

10 Vous … … du bus. (descendre)

EXERCICE 14 **The perfect tense: reflexive verbs** Complete the following sentences using the perfect tense of the verb in brackets.

1 Mes parents … … … à six heures et demie. (se lever)

2 Ils … … … dans la salle de bains. (se laver)

3 Je … … … à sept heures. (se lever)

4 Mon frère … … … à sept heures et demie. (se lever)

5 Je … … … tout de suite. (se laver)

6 Je … … … après le petit déjeuner. (s'habiller)

7 Ma sœur … … … très vite ce matin. (se doucher)

8 Ensuite, elle … … … très vite. (s'habiller)

★ Can you fill in the gaps?

You use the imperfect tense for three kinds of statement:

– to … what something was like

– to say what you or someone else …

– to say what was going on when …

EXERCICE 15 The **imperfect tense** Use the imperfect tense of the verbs in brackets to say what was going on when the telephone rang.

Quand le téléphone a sonné …

1 je … aux cartes. (jouer)

2 mes frères … (travailler)

3 ma sœur … ses devoirs. (faire)

4 mon père … (lire)

5 ma mère … le repas. (préparer)

6 Constance … la télé. (regarder)

7 vous … des gâteaux. (manger)

8 Et toi, que … -tu? (faire)

EXERCICE 16 Complete the sentences using the verbs in brackets. You will need to use both perfect and imperfect tenses.

1 Il … beau quand nous …
   (faire, sortir)

2 Je … des frites quand il …
   (manger, arriver)

3 Ma sœur … la télé quand le
   facteur … à la porte.
   (regarder, sonner)

4 Jacques … au supermarché quand
   il … ses amis. (être, rencontrer)

5 Les enfants … au foot quand
   Marc … (jouer, tomber)

★ There are two ways to talk about the future.
You can say something is 'going to happen' using the verb … and an … or you can use verbs in the …

EXERCICE 17 **Aller + infinitive** What are they going to do? Replace the present tense verbs with *aller* and an infinitive.

1 Je prends le bus.
   Example: Je vais prendre le bus.

2 Il fait du vélo.

3 Nous mangeons au restaurant.

4 Elle boit un coca.

5 Tu fais tes devoirs?

6 Ils sortent plus tard.

7 Vous arrivez en retard.

8 Elles jouent au tennis.

EXERCICE 18 The **future tense** Put these sentences into the future tense.

1 Nous allons aux Etats-Unis.
   Example: Nous irons aux Etats-Unis.

2 Nous prenons l'avion.

3 Nous arrivons à New York.

4 Louis visite les musées.

5 Il voit les œuvres d'art.

6 Pauline fait de la planche à voile.

7 Elle peut aller chez sa tante.

8 Je vais à l'université après le bac.

8 Irregular verb tables

Infinitive	Present	Perfect	Imperfect	Future
aller *to go*	je vais tu vas il/elle va nous allons vous allez ils/elles vont	je suis allé(e) il/elle est allé(e)	j'allais il/elle allait	j'irai tu iras il/elle ira nous irons vous irez ils/elles iront
avoir *to have*	j'ai tu as il/elle a nous avons vous avez ils/elles ont	j'ai eu il/elle a eu	j'avais il/elle avait	j'aurai tu auras il/elle aura nous aurons vous aurez ils/elles auront
boire *to drink*	je bois tu bois il/elle boit nous buvons vous buvez ils/elles boivent	j'ai bu il/elle a bu	je buvais il/elle buvait	je boirai tu boiras il/elle boira nous boirons vous boirez ils/elles boiront
devoir *to have to;* *to owe*	je dois tu dois il/elle doit nous devons vous devez ils/elles doivent	j'ai dû il/elle a dû	je devais il/elle devait	je devrai tu devras il/elle devra nous devrons vous devrez ils/elles devront
dire *to say*	je dis tu dis il/elle dit nous disons vous dites ils/elles disent	j'ai dit il/elle a dit	je disais il/elle disait	je dirai tu diras il/elle dira nous dirons vous direz ils/elles diront
dormir *to sleep*	je dors tu dors il/elle dort nous dormons vous dormez ils/elles dorment	j'ai dormi il/elle a dormi	je dormais il/elle dormait	je dormirai tu dormiras il/elle dormira nous dormirons vous dormirez ils/elles dormiront
écrire *to write*	j'écris tu écris il/elle écrit nous écrivons vous écrivez ils/elles écrivent	j'ai écrit il/elle a écrit	j'écrivais il/elle écrivait	j'écrirai tu écriras il/elle écrira nous écrirons vous écrirez ils/elles écriront
être *to be*	je suis tu es il/elle est nous sommes vous êtes ils/elles sont	j'ai été il/elle a été	j'étais il/elle était	je serai tu seras il/elle sera nous serons vous serez ils/elles seront
faire *to do;* *to make*	je fais tu fais il/elle fait nous faisons vous faites ils/elles font	j'ai fait il/elle a fait	je faisais il/elle faisait	je ferai tu feras il/elle fera nous ferons vous ferez ils/elles feront
lire *to read*	je lis tu lis il/elle lit nous lisons vous lisez ils/elles lisent	j'ai lu il/elle a lu		je lirai tu liras il/elle lira nous lirons vous lirez ils/elles liront

Infinitive	Present	Perfect	Imperfect	Future
mettre *to put*	je mets tu mets il/elle met nous mettons vous mettez ils/elles mettent	j'ai mis il/elle a mis	je mettais il/elle mettait	je mettrai tu mettras il/elle mettra nous mettrons vous mettrez ils/elles mettront
ouvrir *to open*	j'ouvre tu ouvres il/elle ouvre nous ouvrons vous ouvrez ils/elles ouvrent	j'ai ouvert il/elle a ouvert	j'ouvrais il/elle ouvrait	j'ouvrirai tu ouvriras il/elle ouvrira nous ouvrirons vous ouvrirez ils/elles ouvriront
pouvoir *to be able*	je peux tu peux il/elle peut nous pouvons vous pouvez ils/elles peuvent	j'ai pu il/elle a pu	je pouvais il/elle pouvait	je pourrai tu pourras il/elle pourra nous pourrons vous pourrez ils/elles pourront
prendre *to take*	je prends tu prends il/elle prend nous prenons vous prenez ils/elles prennent	j'ai pris il/elle a pris	je prenais il/elle prenait	je prendrai tu prendras il/elle prendra nous prendrons vous prendrez ils/elles prendront
recevoir *to receive*	je reçois tu reçois il/elle reçoit nous recevons vous recevez ils/elles reçoivent	j'ai reçu il/elle a reçu	je recevais il/elle recevait	je recevrai tu recevras il/elle recevra nous recevrons vous recevrez ils/elles recevront
savoir *to know;* *to know how*	je sais tu sais il/elle sait nous savons vous savez ils/elles savent	j'ai su il/elle a su	je savais il/elle savait	je saurai tu sauras il/elle saura nous saurons vous saurez ils/elles sauront
sortir *to go out*	je sors tu sors il/elle sort nous sortons vous sortez ils/elles sortent	je suis sorti(e) il/elle est sorti(e)	je sortais il/elle sortait	je sortirai tu sortiras il/elle sortira nous sortirons vous sortirez ils/elles sortiront
venir *to come*	je viens tu viens il/elle vient nous venons vous venez ils/elles viennent	je suis venu(e) il/elle est venu(e)	je venais il/elle venait	je viendrai tu vendras il/elle viendra nous viendrons vous viendrez ils/elles viendront
voir *to see*	je vois tu vois il/elle voit nous voyons vous voyez ils/elles voient	j'ai vu il/elle a vu	je voyais il/elle voyait	je verrai tu verras il/elle verra nous verrons vous verrez ils/elles verront
vouloir *to want*	je veux tu veux il/elle veut nous voulons vous voulez ils/elles veulent	j'ai voulu il/elle a voulu	je voulais il/elle voulait	je voudrai tu voudras il/elle voudra nous voudrons vous voudrez ils/elles voudront